ONLY A BLOODY GAME!

The Ins & Outs of Village Cricket

Tony Rossiter

Published by Sigma Leisure – an imprint of
Sigma Press, 1 South Oak Lane, Wilmslow, Cheshire SK9 6AR, England.

British Library Cataloguing in Publication Data
A CIP record for this book is available from the British Library.

ISBN: 1 85058 788 4

Typesetting and Design by: Sigma Press, Wilmslow, Cheshire.

Cover Design: Sigma Press *(cricket ball kindly supplied by John Handley and photographed by Graham Beech)*

Illustrations: Brian Sage

Printed by: MFP Design & Print

Foreword

by Geoffrey Palmer

"A cricketer setting off on tour feels like a schoolboy on the first day of the summer holidays." I don't know much about cricket, but I can remember that feeling. Cricket is a game, and the purpose of games, it seems to me, is enjoyment. If *Only a Bloody Game* is anything to go by, those who play cricket – at any rate, those who play village cricket – have a lot of fun.

Only a Bloody Game is about the grass roots of cricket, where "a common level of incompetence can instil a marvellous feeling of team spirit". Tony Rossiter's heroes are not the players who score fifty runs or take five wickets every time they play. His heroes are the has-beens and the never-will-bes, the unfit and the untalented, those who have little skill but a lot of enthusiasm – players like Basil, who "treated the ball with caution, as if it were an unexploded bomb".

Only a Bloody Game is based on real characters and incidents from the author's long and, by his own admission, undistinguished career as a village cricketer. Written in a lively, easy-to-read style, it combines first-hand experience of village cricket with an affectionate, tongue-in-cheek sense of humour for the game.

I'm sure that anyone with an interest in cricket and a sense of humour will enjoy this book. And since it says almost as much about human nature as it does about the game of cricket, even those who (like me) know little or nothing of the game, should find something here to make them smile.

– Geoffrey Palmer

Preface

"All cricketers are cricketers, none the less so for not being 'first class'" (John Arlott)

In its early days, cricket was a simple country recreation – a game played by farm labourers, artisans and tradesmen, who gathered on the common land to relax and enjoy themselves after the day's work. Since its first recorded mention over 400 years ago, the game has changed almost beyond recognition. I suspect, though, that today's players – and especially, perhaps, those who play village cricket – have more in common with those early cricketers than one might suppose. Some things, I'm pretty sure, have changed hardly at all: the exhilaration every cricketer feels, each spring, when he goes out onto the field for the first game of the season; and the sheer sense of fun.

My aim in writing this book has been to capture something of that exhilaration and that sense of fun. For more than 25 years I have spent almost every Saturday in summer playing village cricket. The book is based on my own first-hand experience, on real characters and real incidents, but I have been concerned less with strict factual accuracy than with making the reader smile. So here and there I have allowed myself the licence of a little exaggeration. And if *Only a Bloody Game* takes the piss out of village cricket and those who play it – and it does – the tongue is firmly, and affectionately, in the cheek.

My thanks are due to everyone who has played cricket for or against The Lee (Bucks) between 1976 and 2002. It is they who have provided the raw material on which this book is based. I should also like to thank Geoffrey Palmer for his kindness in contributing a foreword; Elizabeth Stewart-Liberty, for the privilege of playing on what is, in my eyes at least, the loveliest cricket ground in the whole of England; and Graham Mallaband, for his helpful advice. Some of the material in Chapter 4 originally appeared in the National Village Cricket Championship Annual 2000, published by *The Cricketer.*

Tony Rossiter

Contents

Dedication

To Una and Fred; and, above all, to Edna, who has put up with me and my cricket for more than 35 years.

Chapter 1

Better than Lord's

"Heaven can't be any better than this." The first match of the season and our little ground, high up in the Chilterns, is at its best. The outfield has been mown. The pitch has been cut, rolled and marked out ready for play. The oaks and the beeches are beginning to burst out, and everything is fresh and green.

What village cricketer wouldn't settle for an afterlife of continuous cricket, played not at Lord's, but on a ground like this, deep in the English countryside? Beneath your feet, sweet English grass – and the dog-shit on your cricket boots.

When I first played here, the ground was hidden behind a hawthorn hedge. Then one of our members decided it was getting out of hand. He is a chap who believes in making a thorough job of things, so he set to and gave it a trim. Not so much a short back and sides as a number one. The ground is no longer hidden behind the hedge: there is no hedge. But, already a new hedge has been planted – it has taken root and is filling out nicely. In a few years' time it will be just like the old hedge … until someone decides it is getting out of hand and needs a trim.

Two sides of our ground are bordered by a field dotted with trees: oak, ash, sycamore, chestnut, beech. There, for much of the summer, cows graze contentedly. It's a well-known fact that any cricket ball hit into a field with cows in it is more than likely to land in a cow-pat. One of the laws of nature. The fielder who climbs over to retrieve the ball is then faced with a difficult dilemma. Should he give it a thorough wipe on the grass before he throws it back? Or, should he leave the cow-shit undisturbed? In which case, his own hand will not escape totally unscathed. But, for most players, this is outweighed by the schoolboy-like pleasure to be derived from seeing a team-mate catch the ball and realise, too late, that the palm of his hand is caked with something brown and sticky.

Perhaps we should put the substance to a more practical use. In 1938, liquid cow dung, used to prepare the Oval pitch, helped England to a total of 903 for 7. We should learn from history. Admittedly, our batsmen are not quite in the same class as Hutton and co, but in cricket all things are relative. When a team struggles to get its total into three figures, even a marginal improvement can make all the difference. We have often thought that all we really need in order to show our true potential is a reliable base, a solid foundation on which to build our innings. Perhaps cow-shit is the answer.

As May turns into June, the colours around the cricket field begin to deepen. On a warm summer evening, with the wagtails bobbing up and down on the outfield, a cricketer is as close to nature as he can get. He sits on the pavilion steps, chatting to his friends and sipping his beer. He watches the sun go down behind the old oak trees and breathes in the scent of freshly mown grass. The evening is still and peaceful. Until the cricketer sneezes, and sneezes again and again, overcome with hay fever.

*   *   *

One of the larger local clubs we play against has a beautifully appointed ground – the outfield is more immaculate than the square of most village clubs. There is a large, comfortable pavilion with a first-floor balcony and, in front, a members' enclosure protected by a white picket fence. I remember the first time we played there. We drove in convoy through the main gate, parked our cars alongside the pavilion and got out. Then we humped our cricket bags through the members' enclosure and into the pavilion. A couple of seconds later we were humping them out again, redirected to the club's "other" ground where their third eleven were entertaining us. This was on the far side of a distant hedge. We felt like commercial travellers told to go round to the tradesmen's entrance.

In village cricket, clubs with comfortable, well-appointed pavilions are the exception. Our own pavilion was built by the club's artisans some thirty years ago when, judging by the dimensions of the changing rooms, players were a good deal smaller than they are today. Yet, it is not as small as the wooden shed used by one of the teams we play against. Instead of disingenuously referring to this as "the pavilion", they would do much better to call it "the hut". As the original name of The Bat and Ball Inn on Broadhalfpenny Down, headquarters of the famous Hambledon Club, "the hut" has a distinguished cricket pedigree.

One club we play against uses the village hall as a combined clubhouse, changing room and tearoom. The tea is laid out on a long table down the middle of the hall. At the far end of the hall is a stage cluttered with props used by the village's amateur dramatic society, and – with space at a premium – this doubles as the visiting team's changing room. For a team with prima donnas who like to be the centre of attention, it is an ideal setting. On one occasion, our opening bowlers borrowed a couple of the stage props – a horse's head and a long wooden pole – to re-enact, arguably a shade too vigorously, a mediaeval jousting contest. Perhaps they wanted to prove that their flair for acting was not confined to the cricket field. They were being cheered on by the rest of the team, prancing around in their underwear, when the opposition skipper made an unscripted appearance. I'm not sure what he came for, but he took just one look and disappeared without saying a word. A moral victory even before we had got into our cricket gear.

* * *

One of the queerest grounds I have ever played on is on the south coast. The cricket field overlooks the sea. At least that's what I was told but, for all I know, it may overlook a building site or a multi-story car park. On the day of our match, the countryside for miles around was enveloped in a thick, dank mist. So the scenic attractions were lost on us: we could have been anywhere. It was touch-and-go whether or not to start the game at all but we had travelled a long way, and one of the opposition players who had lived in the spot all his life knew the local weather like the back of his hand. He was quite certain that the mist would lift. And he was proved right – some 24 hours later.

Once we had begun the match, we decided that we might as well continue. We could see from one end of the pitch to the other but, on the other hand, a fielder at square leg could see nothing of the ball at all if it was hit on the offside of the wicket. So fielding was rather like a game of blind man's bluff.

When we went out to bat after the tea interval, the mist closed in and the game meandered along in the dismal half-light. It felt more like a Victorian melodrama, moving towards some murky, spine-chilling conclusion, than a game of cricket. As soon as each batsman was out, he lost no time in getting out of his cricket gear and into his car. Player after player revved up, switched his lights on and disappeared into the mist. Those who were left were glad when the game was over, and after the match there was no fraternising with the opposition. We were just glad to get out alive.

Chapter 2

How to be a Skipper

Anyone who thinks the England captain has a difficult job should try captaining a village team. Just imagine you are the skipper of a typical village eleven. None of your batsmen can be trusted to make it into double figures, your bowlers are about as reliable as the English weather, and your fielders are marginally more athletic than a sack of sawdust. With your collection of has-beens and never-will-be's, your only hope is to outwit the opposition. Tactics is the answer, and they are far more important in a village game than in a Test Match.

Only a skipper who understands tactics can hope to get the best out of his team. Bluff and double bluff is the name of the game. One ploy is to toss the ball to the team's self-proclaimed spinner, who rarely pitches the ball and, when he does, turns it not a millimetre. Oddly enough, this phoney can be the best means of removing a pokey batsman who is committed to defence.

We have a bowler like this. It is rumoured that in 1987, playing towards the end of the season on an over-used pitch, he turned one delivery at least half an inch. But, those who have seen him bowl his "spinners" straight as a die, week in week out, find this difficult to believe. He takes one pace up to the wicket, points his left elbow carefully towards the batsman, and lobs the ball slowly and deliberately high into the air. The longer he has played for us, the higher the trajectory of his deliveries has become. Put on late in the afternoon, with the sun low in the sky directly behind his arm, he can be devastating. It is all a matter of tactics.

A skipper also needs tactical skill to handle his quicker bowlers, especially in a limited-overs match. It takes a tactical

genius to leave the team's carefully preserved opening bowler
to finish the innings by bowling two consecutive overs from
opposite ends.

Keeping an eye on the clock is another tactical imperative.
When your cricket is limited to a Saturday afternoon, every
second counts. Time must not be wasted – unless, of course, the
state of the game dictates otherwise. It can take your fast bowler
a surprisingly long time to walk in all the way from long leg,
hand his sweater to the umpire, and retreat most of the way
back again to start his run up. It is astonishing, too, how
frequently he can lose his run up to the wicket. Many years ago
Jon Snow set a fine example when he deposited a pocketful of
cake crumbs behind his run-up mark. These attracted the atten-
tions of a flock of seagulls. Swooping down and distracting the

batsman, they caused a hold-up of several minutes. A master tactician at work.

The Australian captain Warwick Armstrong ("The Big Ship") was another fine tactician. When Frank Wooley made his Test debut in 1900, Armstrong, always looking for a psychological advantage over the opposition, kept him waiting for a full 18 minutes while he bowled a succession of practice deliveries on the outfield – something that was within the letter of the laws applying at the time. It is good to know that the spirit of cricket, given so much emphasis in the 2000 revision of the laws, was alive and well in 1900.

* * *

The ideal skipper, according to Trevor Bailey, needs to be a natural leader and to have a strong character. But, the dividing line between strong and pigheaded can be very thin. One common condition is the disease, first identified by Ranjitsinhji more than a hundred years ago, known as "bowlomania". Giffen, Australia's captain in the 1890s, suffered from this. When a fellow bowler suggested the advisability of a change, he said, "Do you think so? Perhaps I **had** better go on at the other end."

A variant of the same disease has afflicted skippers since the game began. This is batitis, a condition from which W.G. himself was by no means immune. The disease can strike from an early age: a common symptom is the schoolboy's refusal to give up his bat, despite having been comprehensively bowled.

We once had a skipper who (unlike anyone who had seen him play) thought of himself as an all-rounder, and suffered from both varieties of the disease. He was a left-arm bowler who could be counted upon to bowl one unplayable delivery every season – and one wide every over. "It's all about self-confidence," he would say, as he gave himself another over, and silly mid-on gave himself another yard. As a batsman specialising in air shots, he suffered from an allergy common among village cricketers: antipathy to the straight bat. And, like many village skippers, he never allowed lack of success to affect his judgement.

It is in adversity that a captain's qualities of leadership and man-management can be seen at their best. A discomfited batsman, returning to the pavilion without having troubled the scorers, can have his confidence boosted no end by an agonised cry of "why for fuck's sake did you try to hit that out of the ground?" And when one wicket is needed to win in the last over of the game and mid-off spills the easiest of dolly catches – that is when a hysterical, Victor Meldrew-like shriek of "I don't believe it" can do so much to lift the team's morale.

Above all, a skipper must set a good example. "Wait a minute," said R.W.V. Robins, captain of Middlesex in the 1930s and 1940s, setting his field for a young incoming batsman who was playing his first county game, "this fellow can't hit the ball there, or there, or there." Bluff is part and parcel of the game, and "sledging" may be a fairly recent addition to the cricket vocabulary, but the practice is as old as the game itself.

KEENNESS, ENERGY AND CONSTANT PRACTICE ARE THE HALLMARKS OF VILLAGE CRICKET...

A skipper also needs to be an enthusiast. The Victorian cricketer A.G. Steel saw it as a captain's duty to inspire his team, to set an example of keenness and energy, and to engage his men in constant practice. Keenness, energy and constant practice are the hallmarks of village cricket – if you mean keenness to avoid unnecessary exertion, the energy to dash off the field at the slightest hint of rain, and plenty of practice in the bar. An excess of zeal is regarded with deep suspicion. But, some first class cricketers are not so different: neither Ian Botham nor Geoff Thomson was renowned for devotion to practice. Both preferred fishing to bowling in the nets. And yet, the two sports are perhaps not as far apart as one might suppose: one of our slow bowlers compares the art of bowling to the art of catching fish. "You must have plenty of ground bait," he says but, unfortunately, he is much better at spreading the bait than he is at providing the hook.

A captain also needs his share of luck. Geoff Boycott may say that a batsman makes his own, but how much village cricket has he played? When did he have to cope with a batting strip that looks more like a potato patch than a cricket pitch? And an umpire whose eyesight and hearing is marginally better than the scarecrow's in the adjacent field?

Any village cricketer knows that luck is an intrinsic part of the game: the chorus of "hard luck", as a batsman returns to the pavilion without having over-exerted the scorers, is an integral part of the proceedings. And an opening spell from our fast bowler would not be the same without that "lucky bastard" muttered beneath his breath as the batsman plays and misses just outside the off stump. In his excitement, he forgets that the chances of any snick being held by our slip fielders are infinitesimal

*　*　*

Many village skippers have their teams chosen for them by a selection committee – like A.C. Maclaren when he captained England against Australia in 1902. Maclaren's baleful comment, on seeing the team-sheet for the fateful fourth Test, has been echoed over the years by countless village skippers: "My God, look what they've sent me."

A selection committee that meets in mid-week can help its cricket-mad members to get from one weekend to the next without cracking up. And, with no game to distract them, its members can give their undivided attention to the important – and often far more enjoyable – business of talking cricket.

Other clubs eschew selection committees in favour of the Captain Mainwaring school of leadership. At such clubs, the same skipper has often been in charge for as long as anyone can remember. He has a strong belief in democracy: it is given an airing once a year at the AGM – provided it does not interfere with his ability to control everything and everyone.

Autocratic, command-style captains have always been part of the game. William Clarke, founder of the famous All England Eleven, was an early example. Warwick Armstrong habitually ordered his men to be in bed by 11 o'clock – while he stayed up into the early hours taking "medication" for his malaria: he was an agent for Buchanan's distillery. "Do as I say, not as I do" is a maxim favoured by many village skippers.

Jardine's regime during the bodyline series of 1931/32 was run with military-style discipline, his one concession to democracy being the absence of saluting. Another imperious skipper was Lord Hawke who, as captain of Yorkshire in the 1890s and 1900s, did much to improve the financial security of professional cricketers. Paradoxically, he is probably best remembered for his instant sacking of the slow left arm bowler, Peele, whose unorthodox manner of watering the outfield at Headingley had earned his disapproval.

Our team would not have taken to Lord Hawke. After pre-match refreshment, a long afternoon in the field would be unbearable without our two old oak trees on the boundary's edge, offering ideal cover for a full-bladdered fielder whose urgent sprint towards the trees at the fall of a wicket is much faster than any attempt to save runs.

In our club, team selection is an uncomplicated business. When you do not have eleven players, who to leave out is not a problem. The challenge is to find eleven men who are prepared to turn up. Whether they can play cricket is of secondary importance.

* * *

Tactical ability, leadership, enthusiasm and luck – these, according to the experts, are the qualities every skipper needs. But the experts have got it wrong. The first attribute of an effective village captain is possession of a telephone, combined with a willingness to run up huge bills in his efforts to assemble a team. The second is an ability to persuade, cajole, enthuse, flatter, con, bribe, threaten, blackmail or do anything else he needs to do to produce eleven men who can pass for cricketers. A farmer who used to turn out for us provides a good example of the skipper's headaches. He was frequently unavailable due to haymaking or "combining," but would be able to play, he would always add, if it was raining.

On one occasion, our captain excelled himself. We were in the field on a hot afternoon. After an hour or so's play, a tray of drinks was brought out – 15 glasses, as usual – one for each of the 11 fielders, the two batsmen and the two umpires. When all the glasses had been taken, one fielder was left without a drink. It was only then that we were discovered to have taken the field not with 11 players, but with 12. Matches between teams of unequal size were common in cricket's early days, but our extra man owed more to our skipper's arithmetical genius than to his sense of history.

The toss of a coin, a seemingly fair way to determine who shall bat and who shall bowl, presents the under-prepared skipper with a difficult choice. If he has done his homework, he will know that the heads side of a coin is a thousandth of an ounce heavier than the tails side and is, therefore, more likely to fall undermost – making tails the scientifically correct call. But, since at least a thousand tosses of the coin are needed to demonstrate the validity of this theory, few captains live long enough to reap the benefit.

* * *

Any captain can do a great deal to lose the game even before the toss-up. All he has to do is to take at face value anything the opposition skipper says to him. "We're a bit weak today … some of our key players are at a wedding." This probably means that the opposition have only two lethally fast bowlers instead of three. And since one is more than enough to run through our team, the difference is academic. Be wary, too, of the opposition skipper who suggests dispensing with the toss and allowing you to bat – on the grounds that he has a very weak team and would like to make a game of it. Of course, he may be telling the truth: strange things can happen on a cricket field. More probably, he has two match-winning bowlers up his sleeve and a dinner party that he will only be able to get to if the game is over by teatime.

Any experienced skipper of a village team will hope to lose the toss. Winning it, oddly enough, puts him in a no-win situation. His batsmen want to bat and his bowlers want to bowl. If things go wrong – and there is every chance that they will – it will all be put down to the skipper and his absurd decision to bat (bowl), when it was perfectly obvious to everyone else that the only sensible thing to do was to bowl (bat). Things are much easier if you lose the toss: you can put all the blame on the flip of the coin.

So, if you have the misfortune to win the toss, keep the news to yourself – unless, by some unforeseen chance, you should happen to win the game. In this unlikely event, you can reveal your decision to bat/bowl over a pint in the pavilion afterwards: proof of your tactical genius.

Writing out the batting order might seem a straightforward task. But whatever order you decide upon will be unpopular with someone – and with eleven batting positions to fill, you have an excellent chance of upsetting your entire team.

Some players believe that they have a God-given right to open the batting, even if they have spent an entire season trying to get off the mark, whilst others are convinced that luck will desert them if they do not occupy their customary place in the batting order. An average of five may not provide unequivocal proof that number three is the batsman's "lucky" position. But, in cricket, everything is relative. Then there is the nervous type who has not had the chance of an innings for some weeks. So you carefully reconstruct your line-up so that you can slot him in higher up the order. Only when it is time for him to bat does he tell you that he would feel much happier in his usual number nine position. Now and again, someone may murmur selflessly, "Put me anywhere, skip." This might seem a like a godsend, but it should not be taken too literally. "Anywhere" does not mean number eleven.

The truth of the matter is that in village cricket the batting order is an irrelevance. When you know that X will be bowled by the first straight ball he receives, it really does not matter very much whether he goes in first or last. And when the difference in skill between your best and your worst batsman is the difference between a bat hung out to dry outside the off stump and a hoick to cow-corner, you can safely reverse the order without anyone noticing the difference.

The inexperienced skipper pores over his batting line-up for days on end, mixing his sloggers and plodders so that he is prepared for every eventuality. On paper, it looks perfect; it is only on the pitch that the flaws become apparent. Long experience has taught me that the more carefully constructed the batting order, the more certain it is to come unstuck. When all your batsmen are equally capable of self-destructing, it is impossible to predict which, if any, of them will get some runs. Since run-getting is a lottery – pure and simple – why not apply the same principle to your batting order? Drawing lots out of a hat is as good a method as any.

* * *

Where to put the fielders? That, perhaps, is the biggest problem for the skipper of the bowling side. However, the word "fielders" should not be taken too literally: the word implies an ability to field the ball, which may or (more likely) may not exist. Of course, you can hide the odd player whose attempts to field the ball put you in mind of a rabbit chasing a fox. You can put him in one of those positions, such as mid-on, to which the ball hardly ever goes. But when you have to hide an entire team, your ingenuity is stretched. It is astonishing, too, how, as soon as you fill an apparently redundant position with a purely decorative fielder, he suddenly becomes a magnet for the ball.

A few seasons ago the youngest member of our team was fielding at mid-on when, in the final over of the match and with the opposition's last pair at the wicket, he was offered the softest catch imaginable. He stood transfixed, like a rabbit caught in a car's headlights, as he watched the ball go in a gentle arc from the bat to his hands, and from his hands to the ground. However, the following season one of our most senior players, also at mid-on, contrived not only to miss an equally soft catch but to make such a hash of it that he ended up spread-eagled on the pitch, with the ball landing on the most sensitive part of his anatomy. It was only when we had managed to stop laughing that we could get him up onto his feet and help him into the pavilion. It takes a lot of experience to turn a simple catch into slapstick farce.

An experienced player can always find an excuse for a dropped catch. If there is the slightest hint of sunshine, it is the glare of the sun that prevents the catch being taken. If, on the other hand, the sky is grey, the dropped catch can be put down to the dark background of trees that prevents the player from sighting the ball until it is too late. If there is any suspicion of rain in the air, the wet ball and/or the slippery playing surface must be to blame.

On days when none of these excuses is even half-plausible, something more inventive is called for. One of our players, someone for whom the phrase "decorative fielder" might have been invented, invariably has his view of the ball obscured at the critical moment by anything from a swarm of bees to a passing pigeon. This "cricketer" finds chatting to the umpire a far more attractive proposition than fielding the ball. On taking the field, he makes a beeline for the square leg umpire, whom he immediately engages in conversation. Any request from the captain to move elsewhere falls upon deaf ears. Many a skipper unfamiliar with his technique has given up the attempt, and has allowed him to stay on the same spot of grass for the entire innings, fielding at square leg to one bowler and extra cover to the other. When this fielder has exhausted his reminiscences – and the umpire – and he spots a spectator on the boundary, he unobtrusively drifts out deeper and deeper until he is close enough to strike up a conversation. From this position, casting only an occasional glance towards the middle, he passes the time of day with someone who, like him, prefers talking about cricket to playing the game. He rarely stops the ball from going over the boundary; but he is in an excellent position to retrieve it after it has gone past him into the adjacent field.

*   *   *

Any village skipper knows that what happens on the field of play is the easy bit. After all, it does not take a genius to write out a batting order or to decide which bowlers to put on. When all your batsmen are equally incompetent and you only have two half-decent bowlers, these decisions are not difficult.

The real business is done before the game begins. "Has the pitch been marked out? Who's doing teas? Has someone switched the urn on? Where are the umpires' coats? Who's seen the boundary markers? Where's the sawdust? Do we have a match ball? Has anyone seen the bails?" This is when the skipper's organisational skills really come into their own.

In well ordered clubs the pitch will have been marked out hours before the start of play. But for many village teams a frantic, last minute search for whitewash, brush and marking frame are the normal prelude to a match. This custom has its own particular charm yet, inexplicably, it is not always appreciated by an opposition skipper eager for a prompt start.

At the beginning of the season, our tea rota is a fine thing. Before the first match is played, no one has any problems with it. It is only as the dreaded day looms ever closer, and the need to convert a name on the noticeboard into sandwiches and cakes can no longer be ignored, that the victim begins to have second thoughts. Every player faces the same awful choice: to grit his teeth and see to the ghastly business himself; or to grit his teeth and *try* to persuade wife/partner/girlfriend/sister/mother/daughter to do it. Either way, it is an unattractive prospect.

If he goes for the do-it-yourself option, he faces a morning spent maniacally dashing around the supermarket, a lunchtime of sandwich-making, and a frantic ten minutes before tea trying – and failing abysmally – to reconcile his fielding duties with his need to put out cups and saucers, cut up sandwiches, fill up the teapot, put out the cakes, etc, etc, etc. Any player who has to prepare tea always finds that his team is in the field first. It is Sod's Law. And when the game is over, while the rest of the team are propping up the bar, he will finish the day at the kitchen sink, washing up cups and saucers and vowing never to do it again.

However, any player who plumps for the alternative of female assistance soon discovers that this, too, is no easy option. First, there is the sheer amount of effort involved. Persuading her to give up the best part of Saturday to making cricket teas requires a concerted campaign of attack, with careful planning and perfect timing. And if the campaign succeeds, there is a second – equally compelling – drawback: the retribution that is bound to be exacted. For anyone who allows herself to be persuaded to make cricket teas can be counted upon to ensure that the debt is not only repaid, but repaid with interest. So the tea-making will be dragged up again and again throughout the season, and dwelt on at length whenever the unfortunate player needs to be reminded to put up shelves/mow the lawn/decorate the living room/wash the car. Is it really worth it?

Umpires' coats, sawdust, boundary markers, ball, bails – simple, everyday things the skipper needs, week in week out, for the game to run smoothly. Odd how every one of these things habitually goes missing at the very moment it is needed.

The umpires' coats should be on their peg in the changing room. But this, of course, is the one place where it is hardly worth looking. They are far more likely to be at the bottom of the kit bag, hidden beneath a pile of pads. Or in the boot of the skipper's car, or perhaps among the towels in the kitchen. But most likely they will be behind the bar, resting on top of the beer barrels. When, eventually, they are located, it is pretty clear that they have been used as makeshift overalls by mechanics from the nearby garage.

The sack of sawdust should be in the corner of the mower shed. It was seen there last Saturday, the hottest day of the year. Yet today, when play is interrupted by rain, and the skipper is faced with the absolute refusal of his bowlers to operate without it, the stuff is nowhere to be seen. The boundary markers should be in their box in the shed, but that is the one place where you can be certain they won't be found. Perhaps they were left out on the ground after the last match? If so, the chances are that they have either been purloined for firewood or used by passers-by as a handy scraping tool to remove mud – or other, more unpleasant, substances – from their shoes. The match ball, at least, is safe. The skipper, who purchases the stock of balls and keeps them securely at home, brought it to the ground himself. He put it somewhere safe while he looked for the umpires' coats – but cannot quite remember where.

If umpires' coats, sawdust, boundary markers and match ball can all go missing, what chance is there of finding a small but essential piece of equipment like a bail? Hardly a week goes by without an umpire arriving in the middle to find no bails either on the top of the stumps or in the pocket of his coat. There then follows a familiar ritual: first, a shout to the boundary which is either inaudible or incomprehensible; then, a brisk walk in the direction of the pavilion, sometimes (depending on the age and disposition of the umpire) turning into a trot; and finally, a wait of several minutes while a search is instigated. Eventually the bails are discovered. The window sill of the loo is always a good place to look. So the game begins, and the skipper can relax.

Chapter 3

How to be an Umpire

"Ignorant, incompetent, crude and partisan" was how one cricket historian described umpires in the early 19th century. Two hundred years later, and village umpires are doing their best to uphold the principles that guided their forebears. "Two umpires shall be appointed, one for each end, to control the game with absolute impartiality", is what the laws say. But every Saturday in summer, in hundreds of villages up and down the country, umpires work hard to prove they are not "one for each end," but one for each team.

In some village clubs it is the groundsman who, by tradition, acts as umpire. Indeed, he may consider it the most important of his perks. Because whatever the players might think of his pitch, it is the groundsman's pride and joy – and out in the middle, he is in the best possible position to give it the protection it needs. Better still, he can prevent the game from even starting.

The last thing the groundsman umpire wants is for his pitch to be spoiled by a game of cricket. He is adept at finding excuses for not playing. Every year, the first game of the season is put off for as long as possible as he trots out the same old excuses: there has never in living memory been a wetter spring; the ground has never been as unfit for cricket at the beginning of May; the grass is far too soft to get the mower on without cutting up the pitch; he knows that the players will not want to risk spoiling the square for the rest of the season. But, however hard he tries, he cannot delay the evil day forever. When, finally, he is made to see at first-hand how impossible it is to force the stumps into the ground, he knows that the game is up. He has to admit, albeit with as little good grace as he can muster, that it might just be dry enough to play.

In September the groundsman umpire is ready with a different set of excuses. A whole series of mysterious processes must be carried out before the bad weather sets in: scarifying, hollow-tyning, spiking, loaming. The average player's understanding of these words is on a par with his ability to execute a perfect cover drive. But he knows that the groundsman must be allowed to prepare the pitch in exactly the same way as he has done for the last fifty years. He realises that groundsmen are sensitive souls; and that any hint of criticism will help neither the team's prospects of play nor his own batting average. So if their team has a groundsman umpire, the players soon learn to treat him with kid gloves; and to accept that cricket in September is played only in heaven.

During those few weeks when he cannot prevent his pitch being used for a game of cricket, the groundsman umpire will stand in the middle, ostensibly to umpire. However, getting decisions right is much less important to him than protecting his pitch. He derives his pleasure from bawling out any bowler whose follow-through comes within a mile of the danger area and any batsman who uses the back of his bat to hammer down the pitch. Any player foolish enough to provoke him soon lives to regret it. He may be more of a groundsman than an umpire, but the umpire will rise to the fore to exact swift retribution for wrongs inflicted on the groundsman.

In many village games, it is the players of the batting side who take it in turns to umpire. Assembling eleven men who can be passed off as cricketers is difficult enough; finding a twelfth to act as umpire is often out of the question. With two batsmen at the crease, two men padded up ready to go in, and one man keeping the score, there should be six potential candidates. But where are they?

Most village cricketers do not worry overmuch about perfecting their batting technique, but the technique of umpire-avoidance is a different matter. Every player knows that constant practice is essential if he is to hold his own against cut-throat competition. So he spends hour after hour learning his craft, honing his skills, and looking for new ways of out-manoeuvring the skipper. But, more often than not, he ends up falling back on the same old ruses: intense discussions with the solitary spectator in the farthest corner of the ground; a suddenly discovered problem beneath a car bonnet; a long stroll around the boundary, well out of earshot of the skipper; a domestic problem that has to be sorted out, urgently and at length, on a mobile telephone; and – the oldest stalwart of all – a compelling need to spend time in the lavatory.

By definition, player umpires never have a proper understanding of the Laws. They fall into three categories: those who answer every appeal in the Dalek-like monotone of a robot programmed to pronounce the same two words over and over again – "Not Out, Not Out, Not Out, Not Out"; those who employ a rota system for their decisions, allowing, say, one appeal in three; and, finally, those who regard umpiring as an opportunity to exact vengeance for all those idiotic decisions which, season after season, have kept their batting average in single figures. This type of player umpire does not worry about provoking similarly biased decisions when he is at the crease. He realises that the decisions given by his fellow players are a lottery. He knows from long experience that he has every chance of being given Out when he is Not Out. So, he gets his retaliation in first.

Playing hide-and-seek, week after week, with players reluctant to take their turn at umpiring is not much fun for the skipper. So he may turn in desperation to an increasingly rare phenomenon: the grandfather umpire. Fifty years ago, he played village cricket and knew as much – or, more accurately, as little – about the Laws of the game as any other player. Once, long ago, he saw Hutton bat – an experience he has neither forgotten nor allowed anyone – else to forget. That intimate acquaintance with first class cricket has made him an infallible expert on every conceivable aspect of the game. His chances of getting a decision right (or, for that matter, wrong) are just as good as anyone else's. And the middle of a cricket pitch is not a

THE TECHNIQUE OF UMPIRE AVOIDANCE ...

bad place for an old man to spend a summer's afternoon. If it is a hot day, he can even close his eyes from time to time at square leg, knowing that the wicket-keeper's occasional bellow of "How's that?" as he removes the bails with the batsman's back foot hovering around the edge of the crease, can be relied upon to wake him up.

A father umpire can be a safer bet. In fact, a father-and-son combination can be unbeatable. If the son bowls, the father will get the wickets for him. If the son bats, the father will protect his wicket. Protecting a son's wicket traditionally consists of declining, on principle, all LBW shouts and all appeals for catches behind the wicket; but some fathers take things a stage further. One I know routinely turns down catches if the fielder's hands are in contact with the ground – on the basis that the fielder may have allowed his fingers to splay open and let a blade of grass momentarily brush the ball before the catch was secured. The batsman, he insists, must be given the benefit of the doubt. Curiously enough, this principle is applied rather less rigorously when his son is bowling.

Father umpires have been cherished – and feared – for as long as cricket has been played. Some years ago one turned down a loud and confident appeal for a catch at the wicket against his son who, knowing that he had touched the ball, started to walk. "Not out!" shouted the umpire, whereupon the wicket-keeper, seeing that the striker was out of his ground, hurled the ball at the stumps. It missed and went to the boundary. "Were those byes?" shouted the scorer. "No," roared the umpire, "runs!" There have been many variations on the same theme: a hundred years ago, one of the deadliest combinations was the vicar who bowled and his churchwarden who acted as umpire.

As a last resort, the skipper may have to turn to the most unpredictable umpire category of all – the spectator umpire. One such umpire in a village match some years ago caused resentment in the fielding side by a series of doubtful decisions in the batsman's favour. He said nothing, though he was clearly seething with anger. After a while the batsman was clean bowled. "Well, how was that?" asked one of the fielding side. "Not out," said the umpire, marching off the square. "That'll teach you to accept my decisions. Umpire your own bloody matches."

Perhaps my favourite category of all is the moral umpire. He may have been more prevalent in the 19th century, but village cricket has retained some fine specimens. One batsman who remonstrated after being given out, caught off a ball that had hit the ground was told: "If you weren't out, you ought to have been, so get off and hold your tongue." For the moral umpire, the question is not "was he out?" but "did he deserve to be out?"

The moral umpire may have a short memory when it comes to remembering exactly where the ball pitched or precisely where the batsman's legs were when hit by the ball. But he has a long memory when it comes to remembering a player who disputes his decisions. His physiognomy is carefully observed and stored away for future reference, like the mugshot of a convicted criminal.

The moral umpire takes a long-term view of the game. One

batsman who complained at tea about a flagrantly bad LBW decision received an unexpected reply: "Oh, I know you weren't out. Your umpire won the game for you when we last met, and this afternoon I'm trying to square matters."

A sub-category of the moral umpire – almost extinct other than in "beer" matches – is the umpire who believes all cricketers are good-natured, and trusts the batsman to tell the truth when asked questions such as "Did you hit it?" or "Whereabouts did it touch you?" Thus, the length of a man's innings is directly proportional to his lack of moral scruples.

At the other end of the spectrum is the pedant umpire, who applies the Laws rigorously in all their pernickety detail. He is especially good on short runs, fielders encroaching onto the pitch, calls of dead ball, and anything else requiring an encyclopaedic knowledge of the Laws. Usually he is totally lacking in common sense. A couple of years ago I came upon an extreme example of the species: not content with disallowing leg-byes when the striker had made no attempt to play the ball, this umpire disallowed byes for precisely the same reason. John Major once compared one of his troublesome backbenchers to a man in a flapping white coat. Few people know that what he had in mind was not, in fact, a mad scientist, but a crazed pedant umpire.

Whatever the category of umpire, any experienced player knows that it pays dividends to treat him with respect. If he is an assiduous student of the game he may even follow the advice of George Parr, the famous Nottinghamshire batsman: "First of all enquire after his health, then say what a fine player his father was, and, finally, present him with a brace of birds or rabbits ... you will probably do well."

* * *

From cricket's earliest days, the human element in umpiring has been an integral part of the game. LBW is a good example. Few village batsmen have confidence in an umpire's understanding or application of the law. A player who is fed up with being given out LBW off the front foot with his leg well down the pitch may decide to take his guard a yard outside the crease.

VILLAGE CRICKETERS HAVE ALWAYS REGARDED THE UMPIRE AS
THE MOST USEFUL MEMBER OF THE TEAM...

He overlooks the fact that the average village umpire will not
have the slightest idea how far he is in front of the stumps.

Modern technology may have its uses, but it cannot compete
for entertainment with an umpire who is both incompetent and
biased. Real village cricketers have always regarded the umpire
as the most useful member of their team. "They were there to
help their side win – and they did," wrote one early observer of
the game. Well into the 19th century, the choice of umpire was
often based more than anything on a man's fighting weight and
capacity. When the village of Silverstone, in
Northamptonshire, played an away game in the 1850s it was
usual for the team to take along the local pugilist, "Old Brag,"
and some of his companions. They were "lamentably ignorant
of the rules of cricket," but one of them would stand as umpire
"on the count that his decisions were unlikely to be seriously
challenged."

Of course, intimidation does not depend only on physical
prowess. Any village umpire with the right attitude can soon
establish a reputation that will serve him well for the rest of his
career. The appearance of a particular individual as the opposi-

VILLAGE UMPIRES HAVE ALWAYS UNDERSTOOD THE NEED
FOR FIRST-CLASS EYESIGHT AND ACUTE HEARING...

tion's umpire in one of our local derbies is a psychological blow
to our team even before play begins. He is far more dangerous
than their fiercest bowler. Our batsmen know from bitter experience that if they let the ball touch their pads, they are done for.
So, they hop about the crease, determined to keep their legs
well out of the way. This means there is every likelihood of
being bowled by the first straight delivery. There is only one
way to play against eleven men and an umpire – **with** eleven
men and an umpire.

While a captain's role in boosting the confidence of players
is widely recognised, it is not always appreciated just how
much encouragement an umpire can give. On hearing a snick or
seeing the ball hit the pad, a soft whistle, or an expression of
astonishment just loud enough for the bowler to hear, is usually

sufficient to encourage an appeal. The umpire's finger, ready primed in his pocket, can be in the air almost before the appeal is made.

An index finger raised above the head or the words "Not Out", delivered in neutral tones, are the recommended methods of communicating an umpire's decision. But the village umpire knows that a touch of sarcasm or a chuckle of derision can add enormously to his enjoyment. He can make his opinion pretty clear without breaking the one rule he knows and loves: "Never give your reasons for a decision." For he knows that if he is occasionally right in his verdict, it is invariably for the wrong reasons.

Village umpires have always understood the need for first-class eyesight and acute hearing, and present-day players do what they can to keep up standards. Catches claimed after being taken on the half-volley are an excellent way of testing an umpire's eyesight. Players who do this are following good historical precedent: for two hundred years catches were routinely claimed after the ball had hit the ground or been caught with the help of a fielder's clothing. Good hearing is another essential. Some years ago, an umpire in a village match showed no interest at all in an appeal for a catch at the wicket after there had been a clear snick off the outside edge. The bowler's uncomplimentary remarks left him totally unperturbed. "Talk into this ear," he said, turning his head the other way, "I'm stone deaf in the other bugger."

"The white stick comes later," said Sidney Barnes, handing the umpire a dog that had strayed onto the field during a county match against the 1948 Australians. Did he know that the game's very first umpires carried a stave or stick? The batsman had to make contact with this to score his notches or runs. When the method of run-scoring changed, the stave survived for some years as a symbol of the umpire's authority, and could be put to good use if – or, more likely, when – the game became heated. Disputed decisions were commonplace, with teams walking off the field or sitting down in protest, and matches often ended in furious arguments or worse. Once after he had given a decision that decided the outcome of the match, the umpire, Jemmy Dean was chased by supporters of the beaten side who were carrying makeshift weapons. And when Reigate's umpire gave Richmond's last man out, run out, in a match in 1833, the brother of the dismissed batsman was so incensed that he incited the crowd to throw the umpire into the Thames. He was only saved by the timely and robust intervention of some Reigate supporters. Compared to players and spectators in the eighteenth and early nineteenth centuries, today's players are beautifully behaved.

*   *   *

When it comes to disputing decisions, W.G. Grace showed how it should be done. He maintained that he was obliged to argue over doubtful decisions in order to educate umpires who did not have his experience of the game. The older he got, the more certain he became: that the crowds had come to watch him bat – not to see him dismissed by an umpire absurdly subservient to the letter of the laws.

Grace was not alone in his belief that a large crowd should not be disappointed by the early dismissal of a star batsman. In a match at the Hastings festival, the famous umpire 'Bob' Thoms gave Jessop not out from an attempted run out though he was well short of the crease when the wicket was put down. When one of the fielding side complained, Thoms explained patiently: "Sixpenny gate, holiday crowd. Can't disappoint 'em. But near thing, sir, very near thing." You might think that such eccentric behaviour is all in the past. Village umpires know differently.

Chapter 4

The Old Farts

You do not have to be an overweight fifty-something to play village cricket, but someone has to keep up the old traditions. It is sometimes forgotten that Alfred Mynn, one of the best loved of all cricketers, weighed more than 23 stone; and that W.G. Grace, a fine athlete in his youth, was a good 20 stone by the end of his career.

Our village works hard to maintain the standards set by those giants of the game but, regrettably, exercise and healthy eating have taken their toll. Our heaviest player is a mere 18 stone – the same weight as "Ollie" Milburn, the last real heavyweight to play for England. With his rigorous training schedule, based on bars, nightclubs and beer, Milburn was a fine exemplar for any village cricketer. Our man has a little of his jovial rotundity but, alas, none of his skill.

He is a wicketkeeper with a technique based entirely on bulk. Admittedly, his interest in deliveries wide of the wicket is limited but, since his body protrudes a good distance on either side of the stumps, this is less of a handicap than one might suppose.

As a batsman, his overriding aim is to avoid over-exertion. His trademark is a unique, one-handed shot, discovered accidentally a few years ago. Wafting at a shortish delivery just outside the leg stump, he accidentally took his bottom hand off the bat. To his surprise, the ball flew down to the fine leg boundary. He was quick to spot the potential of a shot that, unlike its more orthodox two-handed equivalent, requires movement of neither feet nor body. It suits him perfectly. The only exertion required is a flick of the forearm – like someone playing hoop-la.

If our team has contributed anything to the game's development, it is the use of innovative, one-handed shots. Another
fine example was provided recently by one of our portly opening batsmen. The bowler, an Australian, was fired up and keen
to get at us. When he reached the wicket, the batsman was not
ready. So, he held up his left hand, like a policeman stopping
the traffic. Too late to stop the ball, he nonchalantly dispatched
it one-handedly to the cover boundary. What we enjoyed even
more than the shot was the Australian's mid-pitch riposte: "you
tryin' to take the piss, mate?"

     As for bowlers, we have more than one whose mobility is not
unlike that of "Old" Lillywhite, the famous "Nonpareil Bowler."
Reprimanded by his captain for declining to take a hot return
catch, Lillywhite responded in an aggrieved tone: "Look here
sir, when I've bowled the ball, I've done with hur, and I leaves
hur to my field!" An admirable sentiment. Its only snag is its
assumption of fielders who can field.

* * *

Forget claims that cricket is humiliating for those who are no good at it: village cricket's whole *raison d'être* is to cater for those who are no good at the game. If there is one thing that every village cricketer knows, it is that a common level of incompetence can instil a marvellous feeling of team spirit.

To any village cricketer, the advantages of a heavy fielding side are obvious. A few extra pounds of flesh can take a lot of the sting out of a hard ball travelling at speed. The greater the circumference of the stomach, the better: if there is a large area of flab for the ball to hit, it is less likely to penetrate the field. And a fat fielder can take the pace off the ball much more effectively than a skinny one, since the excess flesh acts as a cushion and deadens the impact (beer bellies are especially good for this). Warwick Armstrong, Australia's captain after the First World War, set a fine example in one game at Leicester. Fielding in the slips, he failed to take a straightforward catch; but the ball hit him on the top slope of his stomach, ricocheted past his nose, went several feet in the air, and was comfortably caught by the keeper.

THE ADVANTAGES OF A HEAVY FIELDING SIDE ARE OBVIOUS...

A heavy man is also likely to be stockier, with short legs that take him closer to the ground, thus reducing the distance he has to reach down when it comes to ground fielding. He also moves around the field more slowly – an advantage when the pace of the game needs to be slowed down. Sri Lanka's Ranatunga showed how excess poundage could be used to avoid unnecessary exertion and to set an ultra-slow rhythm for his fielders. Any village skipper understands the value of placing his heaviest, slowest player on the boundary at fine leg, and requiring him to walk the entire length of the ground at the end of each over.

Crucially, a heavy man is less likely to be able to get out of the way of the ball – especially if he is old as well as heavy. Age, of course, is relative. Our club's youth development policy is tailor-made for the over-fifties: any newcomer not drawing a pension is asked to field at cover point. With a geriatric mid-off and a point with the figure of Pickwick, everything in front of the wicket on the off side is his.

For anyone who aspires to keep up the real, age-old traditions of village cricket, the right kind of diet is essential. Sadly, seeing as the first class game has lost its way, no wonder county cricket is struggling to survive. In recent years, only Mike Gatting made any serious attempt to set the right kind of example. He accumulated steadily throughout a long career. Sticking to the same rigid diet, game after game after game, must have required enormous self-discipline. But Gatting stuck to the task, and the results were there for all to see. The figure spoke for itself.

* * *

If corpulence has always been part of cricket, so has old age. Has any institution ever been as safe from accusations of ageism as MCC? W.G. Grace played his last game at the age of 66. At precisely the same age, a friend of mine scored his first ever century – thereby ruining the reputation (for slow scoring and single-figure innings) he had painstakingly built up over almost fifty years. But at 66 he was a stripling compared to Charles Absolon, a cricketer in and around London from 1826 until 1897, who took 209 wickets when he was 76 and played his last game at the age of 80. The early cricketers recognised the value of older players. When the Wealden villages of Withyham and Hartfield played each other in 1752, every member of each team was over 60. That is one record our team is determined to emulate, and with several of our players already in their sixties, it is only a matter of time.

One team we play against used to have an octogenarian opening batsman – small, shrivelled, with an obdurate defensive push – very perpendicular – that would keep our fastest bowlers at bay for an entire innings. It was useless appealing against this batsman unless the stumps had been demolished. Umpires invariably gave him the benefit of the doubt – even when there wasn't any. He never, ever, walked. He belonged to the old school of cricketers: he took the view that since he was bound to be given Out from time to time when he was Not Out, it was only fair to redress the balance by staying in when he should have been given Out. But since he was only ever given Out when he really was Out, this line of reasoning conveniently coincided with the delight he took in getting up the noses of the opposition.

There is a lot to be said for old players. When our team is out for less than a hundred, they can recall the days when, with an undulating pitch and an outfield of impenetrable long grass, fifty was an exceptionally high total. And the player who complains about the size of the changing room can be be reminded that in the club's early years there was plenty of space to change – beneath the hedge in the adjacent field.

Older players are more likely to understand what cricket was like in its early days. They can provide a useful antidote to those who think that standards of behaviour are not what they were. With gambling an integral part of the game throughout the 18th century, "win at all costs" was the golden rule. Matches were often played in front of large, inebriated crowds standing to win or lose substantial sums of money, and arguments and fisticuffs were commonplace. England's Barmy Army aren't in the same class. Needle matches between local rivals have always had the gentility of a military skirmish. When it comes to bad behaviour, today's cricketers have a lot to learn.

An older player can be the perfect role model for the younger members of a village team. Everything he does can help to set the right kind of example: his late arrival at the ground on match days; his total abstinence from net practice; his unfettered eating and drinking habits; his rigorous avoidance of anything resembling hard work; the effortless air of lethargy he brings to everything he does; and, above all, his sheer bloody-mindedness. He is the embodiment of those character-building qualities for which cricket has always been known.

In the modern world, energy-saving is vital, and many older cricketers set a fine example. They begin an afternoon in the field by "helping" the skipper to set his field and placing themselves in a position, such as slip or point, where the need to run for the ball is much reduced. This is especially important after a heavy tea, when some positions outside the skipper's line of vision can even provide an opportunity for a gentle siesta. If, on occasion, they do need to run after the ball, they do so with such exaggerated sluggishness that any nearby fielder who is marginally less slow-moving feels obliged to take up the chase. When batting, they confine themselves to defensive prods, singles that can be walked, and – if it is a good day – the occasional four.

Any batsman who tries to get an older partner to run is unlikely to survive long enough to try it a second time. Injuries, real or invented, can be used to dissuade an over-enthusiastic batting partner from attempting an easy run. And many older players suffer from deafness, especially when their batting partner calls for a sharp single. This can be doubly useful, first enabling him to avoid over-exertion, and then allowing him to pretend not to hear his partner's oaths as the latter passes him on his way back to the pavilion – run out by a mile after he has been left stranded in the middle of the pitch.

After the game, when the opposition turn out to be a team of bores, one or two carefully selected senior players can be relied upon to give them a run for their money. Droning on and on and on, they are particularly useful when it is time to clear the bar and close the pavilion.

* * *

All village teams have a few old farts in their ranks. One of our players is in his forties so, more often than not, he's the baby of the team. He isn't old, but when it comes to farts, he's your man. His habitual preparation for a game of cricket is an evening in the pub. Those of us who have shared a changing-room with him for a few seasons can identify the previous evening's tipple by the intensity of the odour. By general consent, dark mild is the most lethal. The toilet facilities of many village clubs are bog-standard, with the flimsiest of partitions between urinal and loo-seat and loo-seat and changing room. Privacy is not a high priority. When this player spends time in the loo, as he often does just before a game, the sounds and smells are shared by the whole team. It's the most effective means ever invented of getting the team out onto the pitch in double-quick time.

It's not only our players who are old and fat. One of our umpires models himself, albeit unconsciously, on two early cricketers who took to umpiring: Jemmy Dean, whose figure was "like a broad, half-filled sack," and James Grundy, who had a weakness for fat mutton chops and – being unable to bend – used a special stick with clips on the end to pick up the bails. Umpiring in the days before white coats were worn, Grundy was once complained against by a batsman who said that his bulk interfered with his sight of the ball. Umpire Grundy responded by standing sideways – a change that made things rather worse.

It was the game's early heroes who led the way. Alfred Mynn thrived on real traditional fare, his habitual lunchtime snack being two and a half pounds of beef and a quart of beer. W.G., of course, believed in moderation in all things – including temperance. Today, it is village cricketers who are the guardians of the game's noblest tradition. They know that the game will only prosper if it surrounds itself, as Caesar did, with "men who are fat".

Chapter 5

Heroes

In 1968 Garfield Sobers hit Glamorgan's left-arm bowler, Malcolm Nash, for six consecutive sixes. It was a remarkable performance by a cricketer who will never be forgotten: Malcolm Nash is our kind of hero. Our club may not have produced a Botham or a Bradman, but we did produce Basil.

Basil Chilton was a batsman with just one stroke. "Stroke" seems a better word than "shot," which implies contact with the ball. Basil's stroke was a cross-batted slog to leg. His appearance at the wicket, as our perennial number eleven, brought a stupid grin to the face of any bowler who knew him. If he could produce a well-pitched-up ball on the stumps, Basil's chances of making contact were about the same as his chances of being picked for England.

From time to time, however, against all the odds, Basil succeeded in getting bat on ball. On these occasions the ball could go anywhere, from third man all the way round to fine leg. This depended not on Basil's stroke, which was always precisely the same, but on the direction, length and speed of the delivery. Very occasionally, a slowish ball pitched on the leg stump was hit in the direction of midwicket. More often – because Basil was habitually late on his stroke and stepped away towards square leg as he played it – the ball would end up in the hands of mid-off.

But, on one red-letter day things were different. We looked to be edging towards victory when disaster struck. An over-confident middle-order batsman, who seemed to have everything under control, holed out on the square leg boundary. His replacement was out first ball, LBW to a slow one that, according to the batsman if not to anyone else who saw it, pitched outside the leg stump. Then we had the kind of classic run-out, with both batsmen stranded in mid-pitch, in which our team specialises. This was a double calamity: not only did it remove the one batsman who had any realistic hope of scoring the four runs we needed for victory; but it also left our number ten at the non-striker's end, and the incoming batsman (Basil) to face the bowling. With four deliveries left in the over, we had once again snatched defeat from the jaws of victory.

Or had we? What happened next has become part of our club's folklore. The bowler bowled; Basil played the only stroke he knew; and the ball sailed back over the bowler's head, bounced once and went over the boundary for four. It was Basil's highest score of the season. And he was a hero.

Basil's habitual fielding position was the fine leg boundary. He could throw the ball a good distance, albeit rarely in the right direction. It would always be flung in with all the force he could muster, irrespective of whether or not the batsmen were attempting a run, or of how far he was from the wicket. He took special delight in hurling the ball in when he had been brought in to field close to the wicket at short fine leg. On these occasions our keeper, still nursing fingers bruised by one of his throw-ins the week before, would make a token effort to discourage a full-blooded throw, holding his hand aloft in a defensive gesture, as much as to say, "Not today, Basil. Please, have mercy."

Basil's throwing technique was unique. Its hallmark was a tremendous wind-up, not unlike that of a baseball pitcher or a javelin thrower. However short the distance between ball and wicket, the wind-up was an essential preliminary to the throw. In fact, the wind-up lasted much longer than the throw. So even when the throw was accurate, there was little chance of a run-out: the batsman was usually home and dry before the wind-up had been completed – let alone the ball getting anywhere near the stumps.

Basil's approach to fielding was circumspect: he treated the ball with caution, as if it were an exploded bomb. His instinctive reaction was to move not towards the ball, but away from it.

Once it became clear that the ball was travelling at a gentle pace, this initial movement was reversed: he changed direction and, if it was not by then too late, ran after the ball, picked it up, and threw it in to the keeper. If, on the other hand, the ball was coming at him hard off the bat and showed no sign of slowing down, he accelerated his initial movement and shied away from the ball – a technique he also used with skiers, for which he had a particular aversion.

On one occasion, however, Basil's habitual approach to catching let the opposition down. It was the last over of an exciting, high-scoring game, with both totals well in excess of 200. The opposition's last pair were at the wicket and the scores were level: one wicket needed to tie the match or – more realistically – one run needed to win. Our skipper recalled his opening bowler to bowl the last over. Three dot balls were followed by a half-volley just outside the off stump. The batsman, seeing his chance, slashed hard. But, he got an edge and the ball flew off the bat, straight as a die, to Basil, fielding (heaven knows why) at point. The ball was on him so quickly that he had no time to get out of the way. He clutched his hands to his stomach: when he removed them, there, resting in the palm of his hand, was the ball. I'm not sure who was more flabbergasted – the batman or Basil.

HE HAD NO TIME TO GET OUT OF THE WAY . . .

There are only two prerequisites for heroic status at our club: total lack of ability; and an absurd, obstinate determination to persevere with the game, season after season after season, long after it has become obvious to everyone that your talents are more suited to tiddlywinks. The lack of class that oozes effortlessly from our team is recognised and rewarded at our annual presentation evening. This is where the best batsman/bowler/all-rounder/fielder picks up a cheap little trophy, with his name inscribed on it, as a permanent memento of his achievement. With talent thinly spread, competition is not exactly cut-throat.

However, there is one exception – one prize over which players are willing to fight tooth and nail. A couple of years ago I, myself, put in a strong challenge. As the season advanced, I steadily gained ground. The more games I played, the greater the lead I built up, and by the middle of August I was uncatchable. It was my finest hour: I had won the most coveted, the most prestigious prize of all. It is awarded to the player who has given his team-mates the greatest amount of entertainment during the season – the "duck" cup.

*　*　*

Our team has produced only a handful of genuine heroes, but there is one who became a legend in his own lifetime. This player got married at twelve o'clock one Saturday morning in June, and (yes, you've guessed it) opened the batting for us at two o'clock that afternoon. He was a steady batsman, who loved batting, and liked to spend as much time at the crease as he could. As things turned out, he probably spent more time at the crease than he did with his wife. Heaven knows why, but his marriage did not last beyond a couple of seasons.

One of our younger players (he has not yet reached forty) has a unique combination of talents: the ability to play an immaculate forward defensive shot with a perfectly straight bat; and the concurrent ability to invariably play down the wrong line. When it comes to getting out bowled or LBW, he is in a class of his own. But all cricketers have their day. In one midweek game, this player – unable to get into our team – volunteered to play for the opposition, who were a man short. The opposition skipper showed his gratitude by inviting him to open the innings.

Our hero walked out to the wicket, took his guard, looked nervously around the field, and then looked up to find himself facing our decidedly quick opening bowler. Young and headstrong, this bowler was not in the best of humours. He was affronted at the indignity of having to waste his opening over on an opener who was not a proper opener. So he bent his back and gave him an extra special welcome. The first ball was short and whistled past his nose. The second was a pretty good length, but pitched a good few inches outside the off stump. I was fielding in the gully and – before I knew what had happened – the ball came off the bat like a bullet, flashed past my right hand, and crashed into the boundary at deep point – the best square cut, bar none, that I have ever seen. I am not sure which was more enjoyable – that magnificent, once-in-a-lifetime, totally out-of-character shot, or the expression on the bowler's face.

Why is it that when a player who is usually hopeless plays for the opposition, he invariably plays out of his skin? That square cut is still talked about years after the event, but our hero has never been able to reproduce it when playing for us. I remember another player, a brother of one of our regulars, who turned out for us when we were desperate for numbers. He was always a liability in the field. To produce that level of incompetence, day-in day-out, must have taken a lot of practice. It was a toss-up as to whether or not we were better off taking the field with ten men. Yet once, when he was surplus to our requirements and he ended up playing for the opposition, he took an absolutely blinding catch, diving and clinging on to the ball on the boundary at deep square leg, to dismiss our best batsman. It just isn't fair.

Another of our heroes has a short body, and legs that are even shorter. This gives him a built-in advantage when it comes to ground fielding. Conversely, he is not much use with catches that are more than three or four feet from the ground. He is a dogged batsman whose only problem is running between the wickets. In order to cover the same distance as anyone else, he needs to move his legs twice as fast – his partner is usually halfway down the pitch on the second run before he has completed the first. This player is never in the slightest danger of being dropped from the team, for he has one unique attribute: an uncanny, infallible gift for sniffing out the ball when it has been hit into the hedge or the long grass and everyone else has given it up for lost. He is like a terrier with the nose of a bloodhound. Cricket balls are not cheap, and over the years he must have saved the club hundreds of pounds. We can't afford to drop him.

Most batsmen have the odd butterfly in their stomach before they go out to bat, but one of our players paces up and down as if he is about to face a court martial. When a wicket falls, and he should be putting his gloves on and making his way out to the middle, he makes a dash for the loo. When at last he emerges, he walks sheepishly out to the wicket, dragging his bat behind him as if he is not totally convinced he will find a use for it. By the time he reaches the crease, he is a nervous wreck. He takes a hasty guard and looks about him suspiciously, as if he is about to negotiate a minefield. Shaping up to face his first delivery, he is full of neurotic energy and his head bobs about like a toffee apple on a piece of string. Of course, this does little for his ability to judge the line or length of the ball and it's a relief to everyone when he's out. Including the batsman.

* * *

Cricket may seem a sedate, gentlemanly game, but appearances can be deceptive. Ever since county constabularies were set up in England almost 150 years ago, police constables have brought law and order to the cricket field. Some years ago, our team was in the field when two uniformed constables suddenly appeared from nowhere. They took up a position on the boundary's edge and scanned the cricket field from end to end, as if they expected to find a dead body waiting to be discovered. Perhaps this was understandable enough, given that most of our fielders are about as mobile as the average corpse. After a few minutes they disappeared into the pavilion, re-emerging a second or two later to walk purposefully out to the middle. The bowler, just getting into his delivery stride, saw them in the nick of time and brought his arm over without releasing the ball. He gave them a dark look, as if to say that, whatever crime they were investigating, interrupting a bowler in the middle of his run-up was a far more heinous offence. The PCs made a beeline for the fielder at cover point. After a short – but lively – discussion, they escorted him off the field and into their car.

As the car sped away, lights flashing and sirens sounding, the game recommenced. When the tea interval came, there was only one topic of conversation. Everyone had his own theory and later, in the pub, it became more and more extravagant as the evening progressed. We felt very let down when the "arrested" player, who had come into the pub unobserved and had unobtrusively rejoined the team, offered to buy a round of drinks. Our questions were waved aside without apology or explanation, and were soon forgotten in a haze of alcoholic amiability. How could we quibble with a player who had made such a heroic contribution to the day's entertainment?

*   *   *

Another of our heroes was a podgy teenager whose boyish face contrasted nicely with his sluggishness in the field. He looked nothing like a cricketer, and appearances were not deceptive. He was a natural, slotting in easily and unobtrusively to our team of unfit, untalented players. He picked up the team ethic of lethargy and slovenliness with effortless ease. A good man in the bar, he was a defensively inclined batsman who played his shots with the deadest of dead bats.

Atypically, he took an interest in the history of the game. His heroes were of the 1950s – not the swashbuckling batsmen idolised by most schoolboys, but the stonewallers. His particular favourites were the South African opener, Jackie "slower than pedestrian" McGlew and Trevor "Barnacle" Bailey, who once (in the Brisbane Test of 1958) took over seven and a half hours to make 68 runs. He was a good man to have in the team if staying in was more important than scoring runs. Nought might seem a lowish score, but it all depends on the context. His noughts may have been no more numerous than those of many other players, but they were made with a lot more style. During a career which lasted no more than two or three seasons, he made some of the most beautiful, most flawless ducks I have ever seen.

On one occasion we had nine wickets down and I was batting with him to save the match. He played the first four balls with soft hands and an angled bat, the handle well forward. Each time, he smothered the ball and took the pace off it. It travelled just a few inches from the bat and dropped down safely onto the pitch. The fifth delivery was slightly quicker, and he inadvertently hit it into the gap between mid-on and square leg. Running between the wickets was not his forte and he avoided it whenever possible; but on this occasion I was a yard or two down the pitch before the ball had been delivered, screaming for a run that would take my determined but inexperienced partner away from the bowling and allow me to play out the last ball of the over to save the match. So he trotted through, rather reluctantly, for an easy single, and I squared up to face the last delivery. The bowler went back to his mark, ran in, swung his arm over and released the ball. It was a slower one, right on middle stump, and I played it with the straightest of straight bats – straight into the hands of silly mid-off. When it comes to playing like a hero, there is no substitute for experience.

Chapter 6

Villains

For the Victorians, cricket and Christianity were more or less the same thing. But Victorian values were not always what they seemed, and from its earliest beginnings cricket has been associated more with riotousness than righteousness. For most of the 18th century it was not so much a sport as an excuse for drinking and gambling, and even in Victorian times cricket had its villains as well as its heroes.

Today is no different. Look carefully at the umpires and the scorers, the groundsmen, the spectators – and at the opposition. Villains everywhere. Even in your own team. Especially in your own team.

A special attraction of village cricket is the villainous umpire, a curmudgeonly fellow whose perverse decisions are designed to get up the nose of as many players as possible. With a few flourishes of the finger or a few barks of "Not Out," he can single-handedly ruin a game of cricket. Whether he is dispatching an innocent batsman, raising his finger with the gravitas of a judge passing sentence on a criminal convicted of a particularly nasty felony, or disdainfully dismissing a confident appeal out of hand, he is equally happy. For him the important thing is to be noticed

Not all umpires are the same. Some derive their pleasure not from eccentric decisions, but from an irresistible urge to bore the pants off as many players as possible. They remind anyone who will listen how much better the game was when they played. The end of an over is the ideal time for an umpire to share his pearls of wisdom with anyone within earshot, but an umpire who is determined to give players the full benefit of his experience can easily slip in a comment or two between one

ball and the next. However, it is in the pavilion, after the game
has ended, that the boring umpire really comes into his own.
This is where he is in his element. He can corner an unsuspect-
ing player or two and treat his captive audience to story after
story, each one more boring than the last.

* * *

Scorers are the backroom boys and girls of cricket. Often they
are quiet, inoffensive souls who watch proceedings with an
eagle eye and record every ball bowled and every run scored –
or almost every ball and almost every run. With their noses
buried in their scoring books, the occasional ball or the odd run

is bound to escape them, and a batsman who returns to the pavilion after counting every painstaking run of his long and monotonous innings can always be relied upon to point out that the figure against his name should be nine, and not eight.

Most scorers pride themselves on the accuracy of the scorebook. The accuracy of the scoreboard is a different matter. Scorers often delegate this task, either to a small boy or to members of the batting side. Small boys are usually very conscientious. It is often their first introduction to the game. A small boy who keeps his eye on the game can have the numbers up on the scoreboard almost before the batsmen have finished running. His alertness and keenness can provide a nice contrast to the lethargy of the players.

A scoreboard entrusted to members of the batting side is a different kettle of fish altogether. The chances are that they will have far more important things to do – things like chatting to their friends, getting a few minutes' shut-eye, or catching up on the race results. It is a strange thing that a batsman who is out in the middle, chasing the runs his side needs for victory, constantly looks towards the scoreboard and shouts to his team-mates to keep it moving…yet as soon as he returns to the pavilion, his interest in the score vanishes and he becomes as deaf as a post. All the shouts in the world cannot persuade him to get out of his chair. So any similarity between the figures in the scorebook and those on the scoreboard is likely to be accidental.

For anyone who wants to re-live the highs and lows of the season, there is nothing better than a browse through the scorebook – provided he is not in too much of a hurry. Deciphering the hieroglyphics can take some time. Now and again, a club may be lucky enough to have a scorer who does the job for an entire season and records every detail in beautiful, copperplate handwriting. More often, the scorebook is a slapdash confection that looks as if it has been walked over by a crab – a mixture of spidery scrawl, crossings-out and strange, inexplicable blotches. A village scorebook would provide fascinating case material for those experts who believe that handwriting is an indicator of personality.

* * *

If cricket is the spectator sport *par excellence* – a game far easier to play from the comfort of the pavilion or a deckchair beyond the boundary – spectatorial skills are not always given the recognition they deserve. Two qualities are prized above all others: hindsight and pessimism. The English enjoy failure, and there are few things the spectator at a cricket match enjoys more than the prospect of failure. Whether he is watching England or his local village team, an experienced spectator can spread doom and gloom through the crowd quicker than a forest fire; all it takes is a few sarcastic words and a barbed comment or two. But it is at the grassroots of the game that pessimism really comes into its own.

Critics' corner is where you will find it. You can't get any closer to the heart of village cricket; this is where the club's little band of supporters, a fine body of men, gathers every week. This is where they chew the cud and develop their critical faculties. To be accepted as a full-blown member of this elite circle, a newcomer must learn that, however well his team are doing, there is always something to criticise. If he looks hard enough, every shot, every ball, every bit of fielding, has something wrong with it. And as a critic, it is his job to find it. He can make useful comparisons between the current players and those of twenty or thirty ago; he knows that the old days were always better, on principle.

Whether the batsman is a slogger or a plodder makes no difference: he can be criticised just as easily. He is the one out in the middle, and if things go wrong, he is to blame. A pokey batsman who stays in his crease and pushes and prods at the ball is an easy target: "He can't go too fast: he thinks he's at a funeral"; "watching him is better than counting sheep"; "he reckons it'll explode if he hits it too hard". However, a batsman who sends the ball sailing into the oak trees can be criticised just as easily. He may get a shout or two of approval, but if he thinks the onlookers are satisfied, he had better think again. They know there is every chance it will go to his head: "He'll not last long. He'll try it again, and that'll be it." And – more often than not – it is.

The critics are always happy to give any fielder within earshot the benefit of their experience. A fielder standing on the boundary line can be given helpful advice ("if I were you, I'd go a bit deeper") and told why the bowler who has just been carted over square leg should never have been put on in the first place. And after he has narrowly failed to stop the ball going over the boundary, a sympathetic comment or two can do a lot to lift his morale: "they shouldn't put you out on the boundary – not at your age".

These days, some of England's Barmy Army add to their enjoyment of the game by wearing silly hats, singing obscene songs and consuming vast amounts of beer. Our supporters are not at all like that. They do not wear silly hats and they do not sing obscene songs.

One of our ex-players fancies himself as a member of the Test Match Special commentary team. He knows that the last thing players and spectators want is to be allowed to watch the game in peace and quiet. So, he treats them like a radio audience, unable to see for themselves what is going on. He keeps up a ball-by-ball commentary, sprinkled with personal reflections and acute, perceptive remarks. So after a bowler has sent down three consecutive wides, our commentator will point that "he's having trouble finding the right line". When a batsman has had his middle stump knocked out of the ground, "he played down the wrong line." And, after two long hops have been followed by a full toss, "he hasn't quite found the right length yet". Surprisingly, the rolled up newspaper that he sometimes uses as a make-believe microphone has not yet been stuffed down his throat.

*   *   *

Some spectators find it tiresome to spend the entire game watching the players; they think it only fair that the players should have to spend some time watching them. A leisurely stroll behind the bowler's arm, just as he is starting his run up to the wicket, is ideal for the purpose. Most village batsmen have enough difficulty seeing the ball, let alone some distant figure beyond the boundary, but for any self-respecting umpire the opportunity to shout and gesticulate to a spectator who is walking along the boundary behind the bowler is too good to miss. While the bowler aborts his run-up, cursing beneath his breath, and the fielders stop walking in and go back out again, all eyes are on the spectator behind the bowler's arm.

Some of the players' partners have got this off to a tee. Two ladies walking arm in arm around the boundary can be relied upon to stop, transfixed – like rabbits caught in a car's headlights – as they get near to the line of the wickets, only to start walking again at the precise moment that the bowler begins his run-up. Perhaps they know that in cricket, timing is everything.

The truth is that cricket is likely to be the last thing on their minds. They may take a passing interest in the game and in the performance of their husband/partner/boyfriend because they know from experience that if he has a bad game, he will be difficult to live with for the rest of the day. But they have not come to watch the cricket. They have come to do the crossword, or finish their paperback; to laze in the sun, or catch up on gossip; and – most important of all – to make sure that when their man says he is playing cricket, then that is what he is doing.

Small children are less of a nuisance. If they run along the boundary behind the bowler, this is over and done with in a jiffy – unless a toddler happens to spot his dad in the outfield. When this happens, the family reunion and the tearful parting that follows, as the toddler is picked up and deposited in the mother's lap, can provide a few moments' respite from the game. Dogs can also be good entertainment value. It is surprising how often a dog running onto a cricket field ignores every player except one; it makes a beeline for one lucky individual. Tail wagging furiously, it shows its affection by jumping up at him, licking his face, sniffing him all over and pressing its nose into unmentionable places.

*   *   *

The groundsman, the most important person in any cricket

club, can also be a villain. With a little tender loving care, he can ensure that the condition of the pitch is just right – not for the batsmen or the bowlers, but for the groundsman. The last thing he wants is a surface that breaks up and leaves him with a mountain of repair work. He knows that a grassy surface will guarantee both an exciting game, with plenty of bruises all round, and – more importantly – an early finish, so he can tidy up the strip and get home in time to catch his favourite television programme.

Every opposition team has at least one villain. He may be a nice enough chap when he is away from the game but, as soon as he gets into his cricket gear, something happens: he turns into an obnoxious prat. The body language says it all. You just know that he is used to playing at a higher level, against higher-class opposition; that he is doing you a favour by turning out at all. After the game, when his team has been beaten, you know, before he opens his mouth, that he will be ready with a string of lame excuses. Perhaps the opener was recovering from flu and was not his usual, solid self; the team's star batsman, who scores a thousand runs a season, was away at a wedding; and the demon bowler was not able to play because he had been called up into the county's second eleven. You can enjoy the feebleness of these stories as you sip your beer, and smile and say nothing.

*   *   *

But the worst villains are found closer to home – in your own team. Team spirit is all very well in theory. But when it comes down to it, what chance is there that eleven players will all get on together? There are bound to be some clashes. As in any family, it is not the big things that cause the arguments. There are no quarrels about religion or politics or the meaning of life. It is the little, everyday things that cause trouble: miserly players, who put off paying their subscription for as long as they can; thirsty players, who see the bar manager's refusal to stock their favourite tipple as a hanging offence; and malodorous players, with idiosyncratic ideas about personal hygiene. Village cricket has them all.

However, it is on the field of play that the team villain really comes into his own, with his natural ability to get up the nose of his team-mates. A common example is the chap who, irrespective of the state of the game or the instructions of his skipper, always plays in exactly the same way. Every team has one, and there is one phrase he loves above all others: "play your own game." When he hears this, he knows that he can stick through thick and thin to the one stroke he knows and loves. Very often, this is a forward defensive prod.

We have a player like this. However short the delivery, he never, ever hits across the line. At school, he was taught to play with a straight bat and he has never forgotten this. He has stuck to this principle throughout a long and unsuccessful career. So long-hop after long-hop goes unpunished, as he keeps his bat perpendicular and pats the ball back to the bowler. He has never quite mastered the knack of turning his defensive prod into a drive. When the state of the game requires quick runs, he keeps his bat straight, blocks ball after ball and sticks to his principles.

His antithesis is the batsman whose only stroke is a cross-batted swish to leg. He has a good eye and, more often than not, he gets bat on ball. If he stays in (admittedly, a pretty big if), he scores quickly. He has never had any coaching in his life and he knows no other way of playing. So when the state of the game requires someone to put the hatches down and stay in, he hits across the line at ball after ball, playing his own game. Every team needs its sloggers and its plodders – thick-skinned players who, regardless of the actual state of the game, will play their own game in their own way. They have a vital role to play: when things go wrong, there is someone to blame.

There is another type of villain, the most deadly of all. For him, getting the better of a team-mate – scoring more runs or taking more wickets – is far more important than winning the game. His only aim is to outdo his rival. If he succeeds in this, he is happy. And if he can go one better and assist in his downfall, he is even happier still. If the catching ability of our team is bad, our running between the wickets is worse. It is the player who manages to hang on to a catch, or to strike up a good under-standing with his batting partner, who is likely to be noticed. So a player who puts down a catch (however easy), or runs out his batting partner, is merely doing what is expected. Even if it makes his day.

Chapter 7

Aggro

"Cricket makes for tolerance and kindly feelings", said A.E. Knight, writing in cricket's golden age before the First World War.

Anyone who has played in a village derby knows how just tolerant and kindly cricketers can be. I'll give you an example. When a new batsman comes out to the wicket, a word or two of welcome can help to put him at his ease. As he takes guard and looks around the field, a quiet comment from the keeper can do a lot to boost his confidence: "not made too many runs this year,

I hear". And as the bowler marks out his run-up, disappearing towards the boundary, a casual remark from the slips can help to settle his nerves: "he's faster than he looks".

With practice, comments like these can be muttered just loud enough for the batsman – but not the umpire – to hear. For maximum impact, they can be timed to coincide with the delivery of the ball. The ideal moment is that instant, just before bat makes contact with ball, when the batsman needs every ounce of concentration.

Forward short leg is well placed to give the batsman an especially warm welcome. He can drop the occasional sarcastic comment from the corner of his mouth while he makes eye contact with the batsman and stares him out. Some short legs like to fix the batsman with an imbecilic grin, as much as to say, "I can see you're not much of a batsman." Others prefer a dead-pan, psychopathic glare. This is a psychological game the fielder is bound to win. He knows that, sooner or later, the batsman will have to divert his eyes away from the fielder and fix them on the bowler.

But the close fielders do not always have things all their own way. A few years ago, a friend of mine was batting against a slow bowler when he played too soon and spooned a dolly catch to the keeper. It went a good way up into the air, and before it came down my friend had time to play a second shot. Determined not to be given out "hit the ball twice", he took great care not to make contact with the ball; and equal care to make contact with the keeper. Solid contact. Perhaps he had taken his cue from W.G. Grace who, batting with his brother E.M. in a Gentleman v Players match, deliberately obstructed the bowler as he went for a straightforward return catch. My friend avoided being give out "caught" or "hit the ball twice". Instead, he secured a place in the club's record book as our first ever player given out "obstructing the field".

When the umpire's finger went up, he set off for the pavilion with as much dignity as he could muster – unlike another batsman I remember. This fellow's technique was unsophisticated, and perfectly suited to his bat: a huge chunk of wood with

which he bludgeoned a quick fifty. He alternated between a
dead bat, played with no backlift and minimal movement of
hands and feet, and a cross-batted thump to leg. Infuriatingly,
the ball always came off the middle of the bat.

His most memorable stroke came after he was given out
LBW. From my position on the boundary at deep square leg, it
looked like a pretty good decision. His front leg was no more
than a yard in front of the crease, and the point of impact was
only a few inches above the knee. After glaring at the umpire's
raised finger for several seconds, he pivoted smartly through
180 degrees and brought his bat round in a perfectly executed
pull, with a fine follow-through that sent the bails flying and
turned the wicket into a heap of firewood. It was a splendid
stroke, but it was too splendid for some people. When we
played the return fixture a year later, the demolition expert was
gone. A sad loss.

This puts me in mind of the time I demolished the stumps. I
have always found the sweep a difficult shot, but a couple of
years ago I finally mastered it: I got bat on ball and swept it
sweetly round, just backward of deep square leg. Sadly, my
follow-through was just a shade too full, and I also swept away
the leg stump. As it happened, both umpires were watching the
ball at the critical moment and could not, therefore, be certain
when or how the wicket had been put down. With the game
finely balanced, I saw no compelling need to enlighten them.
Quite rightly, I was given the benefit of the doubt. As a batsman,
I am a firm believer in always giving the batsman the benefit of
the doubt. Even when there isn't any.

Batsmen who do not walk when they are obviously out are
often ridiculed, but it is batsmen who walk and are subsequently pronounced "Not Out" who look really stupid. I know:
it has happened to me. On the occasion in question, I was skip-
pering the side. There had been some bad blood between the
teams when they had last played, and I was determined to set an
example of good sportsmanship. Too determined. I convinced
myself that I had got a wafer-thin edge to a ball that whistled
past my outside edge and went through to the keeper. Neither

bowler nor keeper appealed, but I took two purposeful strides towards the pavilion. At this point the bowler turned towards the umpire and murmured a very low-key, unconvincing appeal. "Not Out" came the reply in a firm, clear voice. Whereupon I sheepishly retraced my steps, narrowly avoiding being stumped as the keeper hurled the ball at the wicket. Feeling stupid after playing a fatally idiotic stroke is a common enough occurrence for me; feeling stupid after being given "Not Out" was something new.

To walk or not to walk, that is the question. Whether 'tis nobler in the mind to suffer the slings and arrows of outrageous umpires, Or to take arms against absurd decisions, and by opposing end them? The problem is that opposition to absurd decisions does not end them. In fact, it increases them. There is nothing an umpire likes better than the opportunity to put a player who shows dissent in his place. And what better way of doing this than following one absurd decision with another? And another.

When I am out, I usually walk. When the stumps have been

comprehensively shattered by an unplayable delivery, there is not much point in hanging about until the umpire raises his finger. And every delivery that hits the stumps is, by definition, unplayable. When things are tight, though, it is a different matter. I once went out to bat when our team was in a desperate situation: five wickets down and next to no runs on the board. The track was more suited to mountain biking than cricket, and the opening bowler was enjoying himself, peppering us with a succession of short-pitched deliveries. I managed to hang around for a few overs but, before long, the opposition skipper remembered my ineptitude against slow bowling, and tossed the ball to his tweaker. After prodding uncertainly at the first two deliveries, I totally misjudged the third. I misjudged it as completely as any batsman has ever misjudged a ball. I misjudged the length, direction, trajectory, spin – everything. The result was an outside edge, comfortably taken by the keeper. The snick was so loud it was probably heard in the next county. I stayed at the wicket, awaiting the inevitable. But it never came. The bowler had run across in front of the umpire as he delivered the ball, obscuring his view at the critical moment. So although the umpire had heard something, he had seen nothing; and he could not, therefore, give me out.

Staying in when I knew I should have been back in the pavilion did me no good. It made me feel uncomfortable. What was needed was an obdurate, safety-first innings in the tradition of men like Geoff Boycott and Chris Tavare; an innings to make watching paint dry or grass grow seem, by comparison, an interesting way of spending an afternoon. It was the sort of innings for which my repertoire of strokes was ideally suited: forward defensive shots played with a dead bat, interspersed, for the sake of variety, with an occasional backward defensive stroke; little dabs through the slips; gentle nudges around the corner, past backward short leg; and, once I have got my eye in, the occasional full-blooded slice down to third man. Instead, I started to play out of character, to do something I do not usually attempt before August, when the pitch is fast and true. I started to put bat to ball – to hit the ball as hard as I could. I should have known better. The spinner was in his third over when I charged down the pitch, missed the ball, and was stumped by a mile.

*   *   *

Now and again, a batsman survives an appeal for a catch at the wicket when everyone except the umpire is convinced he has hit the ball. One of our players does this at least once a season. "Did you touch it – that one they all went up for?" he is asked when he returns to the pavilion at the end of his innings. His answer is always the same: "I honestly don't know." Of course, no one believes him. A batsman always knows whether or not he has touched the ball. But, we can translate his answer easily enough: "If you think I'm going to admit I hit that ball, you can bloody well think again. I've had more than my share of bad decisions. It's about time I had a bit of luck."

Occasionally, there may be a bit of aggravation between players on opposing sides; disputes between members of the same team are far more common. Take running between the wickets. What other aspect of the game provides so much scope for disagreement between team-mates? Or so much entertainment for the opposition? It is not long since a village match at Camborne in Cornwall had to be abandoned when two batsmen started fighting after a row over who was to blame for a run-out.

By the time two players have played together for twenty years, excelling from time to time with partnerships that get into double figures, they have developed a perfect understanding. Batsman A knows that batsman B's idea of backing up is to stay well behind the bowling crease until A has not only hit the ball but is half-way down the pitch. B knows that he has as much chance of getting blood from a stone as he has of getting a clear call from A. "Yes", "no", "wait", are the calls recommended in the coaching books – but these are long and difficult words, far too complicated for the average village cricketer.

An experienced batsman knows instinctively whether or not a run is "on". Unfortunately, with any pair of village batsmen, the instincts of one are likely to be the exact opposite of the other. The decision – to run or not to run – isn't easy. The batsman has to size up the situation in a flash. He has to take in the positions and the throwing ability of the fielders, and to decide whether he can make good his ground at the other end. That is difficult enough, without worrying about whether or not his partner can get home. He can look after himself. In village cricket, he has to.

A batsman contemplating a run needs to watch the fielders carefully – and his partner even more carefully. One of our players is renowned for his ability to turn any potentially exciting situation into a boring draw. Instead of using the bat to hit the ball, his technique is to allow the ball to hit the bat. In one game a year or two ago, he approached a run-chase with the enthusiasm of a hibernating tortoise. His batting partner became more and more exasperated: for three overs on the trot our hero combined the deadest of dead bats with an uncanny ability to nick a single off the last ball of the over. Drastic action was called for. When he attempted a single off the last ball of the next over, his partner waited until he was halfway down the pitch before he shouted "No!" and declined to leave his crease. But it was to no avail: a poor throw-in combined with the keeper's clumsy removal of the bails before he had the ball in his hands allowed the batsman to survive. This was such an inept piece of fielding that it could only have been a deliberate ploy to keep our dormant batsman at the wicket.

On one occasion I was batting, late in the day in murky light, with our number eleven. Comprehensively outplayed, we were about a hundred runs in arrears. Our only hope was to hang on for a draw. There was no other option – unless you were a number eleven who likes to put bat to ball or, to be more precise, likes to try to put bat to ball. Cricket is always described as a team game, especially by those who do not play it. In reality, it is all about personal glory. Untroubled by any thoughts about saving the game, my partner flung his bat at the first ball he received with all the stylishness he could muster. His bucolic, cross-batted swish might have been designed to minimise the likelihood of making contact. A moment's reflection would have told him that, even if he had succeeded in getting bat on ball, the chances of a catch were a good deal higher than the chances of a boundary. But reflection does not come easily to a village number eleven.

This was not just any old match. It was a needle match against local rivals. For me, as skipper, it was the most important game of the season. The longer my partner was at the crease and the more time he had to get used to the bowling, the more likely he was to get bat on ball. And when that happened, the game would be up. The opposition's only problem would be deciding which one of them should take the catch. I needed to give my partner some skipperly advice, and I didn't want to wait until the end of the over. That might be too late. I marched down the pitch, it was time to put my consensual, sensitive leadership style into practice: "I don't want to lose this fucking match. D'you understand?"

The average player's instinctive reaction to any instruction from the skipper is to ignore it. His natural inclination, reinforced by habit and experience, is to be as bloody-minded as possible. But, the uncharacteristic f-word had its effect. For the first time in his entire life, he began to play sensibly. It was a novel experience. If the ball was on the wicket, he stopped it; if it was off the wicket, he left it alone. I looked on in admiration from the non-striker's end, as our opponents became more and more frustrated. The longer we were in, the more ragged they became. They began shouting at one another, blaming one another for tiny mistakes. It was lovely to see. We played out the remaining overs to end with an undeserved draw. The opposition were totally pissed off. It could not have happened to a nicer team.

*   *   *

For a player to act as umpire while his own team are batting is common practice in village cricket. This arrangement has a lot to be said for it. For one thing, it can provide a great deal of entertainment. Of course, a player standing as umpire may give the occasional decision the opposition do not like, but what is absolutely certain is that he will give plenty of decisions his own team do not like. Take LBW, for example. Has any village batsman ever been known to agree with an LBW decision given against him by one of his team-mates? Disputed run-outs are another rich source of entertainment. It is surprising how many village umpires who religiously give the batsman the benefit of the doubt in any appeal for LBW or caught behind (even when the umpire is the only person on the field who has any doubt), instinctively apply the rule in reverse when adjudicating on a run-out. With no televised action replays to help them, close calls are often decided in favour of the fielding side – especially when the umpire has failed to get into position quickly enough and does not have the faintest idea whether the batsman is in or out.

With the revised laws of 2000, fast or medium-paced full tosses that reach the striker above waist height, as well as slow full tosses above shoulder height, are no balls. But where, exactly, is the batsman's waist when he is crouching down to allow a full toss to pass over him? And where, precisely, is the dividing line between a fast or medium-paced full toss and a slow full toss? Village umpires have had a lot of fun interpreting the new law. In one of our recent matches our opponents were not amused when a high pitched delivery was called 'no ball.' They should have had no cause for complaint – if the call had not been made some seconds after the ball had been well caught by deep square leg. In another match our star batsman was going well against a moderate bowling attack when the umpire failed to call 'no ball' to a medium paced delivery that he ducked under, only to see it land on the top of his stumps. This looked very amusing, seen from the pavilion. Inexplicably, the batsman failed to see the joke.

"Boundary" implies a clear dividing line between what is inside and what is outside. But in village cricket things are seldom as clear-cut as that. The boundary may be a faded line that once, long ago, was white. It may be a dozen or so boundary markers, plonked down at random, with little concern for accuracy or consistency. Or it may be the oldest boundary of all, one the game's earliest practitioners would have recognised: where the outfield merges into the long grass.

With boundaries like these, only the fielder closest to the

ball can know for sure whether or not the ball has crossed the boundary. So a lot depends on the honesty of that fielder. Ninety-nine percent of the time, a player fielding on the boundary gives an honest indication. Just occasionally, however, he scratches his head and decides, with enormous reluctance, that a ball which any impartial observer would have judged a boundary has not quite reached the line. It is sheer coincidence that this happens only when the game is tight and the scores are close.

Chapter 8

How to Get Out

Getting out is easy. Ask any village batsman. The laws of cricket define the ways in which a batsman can be dismissed. However, every village cricketer knows that these are just the tip of the iceberg. They may be the technical ways of getting out, but the underlying causes are altogether different. To get out in a village game, most batsmen do not need any help from the bowler.

Cricket is a simple game. "Stop the good balls and hit the bad ones" is not a bad maxim for any village batsman. After all, he is not up against Glenn McGrath. More than two or three good deliveries an over is the exception. All he has to do is to wait – wait for the one that is short, or wide of the wicket, or over-pitched. It will come, and probably very soon; he can count on it. But the village cricketer is an impatient soul. After all, he only has a couple of hours to build an innings so he can't afford to wait for the loose delivery. The good length ball on the stumps is usually the one he decides to have a go at.

We have one player who believes in putting bat to ball. He claims to have a good look at the bowling first, but his idea of having a good look at the bowling is to play the first ball defensively back to the bowler. Very occasionally, if he is in a really determined mood, he plays the second ball defensively. This is enough to confirm him in the view he had formed back in the pavilion – that there is nothing special about the bowling. So he throws caution to the wind and launches an all-out attack. He puts the full face of the blade to the ball and unleashes his heavyweight bat in a fierce arc. As he brings the bat down, a small technical flaw – which thirty years of cricket have never quite corrected – takes his head high into the air. The result, though, is by no means predictable. Will he be caught in the outfield? Or will he be bowled? Who can tell? It is anyone's guess. All we know for sure is that, one way or another, he will find himself heading back to the pavilion.

*   *   *

Another player has an idiosyncratic method. The stroke he plays is always predetermined. It bears no relationship whatever to the ball bowled. Whether it is short or over-pitched, fast or slow, on the wicket or off it – it makes no difference at all. If, very occasionally, the stroke he plays seems the right way of dealing with that particular ball, this is coincidence, pure and simple. It is all decided in his mind long before the ball reaches him. His method is very simple. Some people paint by numbers, this man bats by numbers. It is a unique system, worked out with great care and precision at the beginning of each season. Every time he goes out to bat, there are slight variations on the same basic theme. But the basis is always the same: numbers.

He uses a simple arithmetical formula. Since he has just two basic shots, a defensive prod (DP) and a big heave (BH), there are just the two components. A typical innings might go like this. First over: 2DP, 1BH, 2DP, 1BH. Second over: 2BH, 1DP, 2BH, 1DP. Third over: 6DP. Fourth over: 6BH. If he manages to survive to face a fifth over, he repeats the same pattern over again. It is a system that can drive a sane bowler mad – very quickly indeed.

There is, however, one basic flaw. The system is designed around an assumption of facing six consecutive deliveries – reasonable enough, given the way he plays. His defensive prod is played with a dead bat and head low over the ball, almost touching the grass. It usually travels no more than six inches from the bat. His big heave is an almighty, cross-batted slog to cow corner. If it connects, the ball soars into the stratosphere and there are only two possible outcomes: either it sails over the boundary or it sails into the hands of a fielder. When he is at the crease, there are three realistic possibilities: a dot ball, a boundary, or the fall of a wicket.

Occasionally, however, the plan goes awry. Perhaps a full-blooded hit to leg does not quite come off and the ball goes off an inside edge down to fine leg for an unpremeditated single. Finding himself unexpectedly at the non-striker's end, the batsman has some difficulty getting his system back on track. And if his partner runs a single or a three so that he is once more on strike, does he disregard the balls bowled while he was at the non-striker's end, and resume where he left off? Or does he count the balls received by his partner as if he had faced them, and play the stroke – DP or BH as the case may be – planned for whatever ball of the over he now has to face? He has never quite made up his mind about this, and so the auto-pilot that controls his innings is thrown out of kilter, with predictable – and disastrous – results.

* * *

One of our players, not in the first flush of youth, is renowned for his madcap running between the wickets. Once he has managed to get bat on ball a couple of times, there is no holding him. Adrenalin flowing, he sprints up and down the pitch as if there is no tomorrow. Once, long ago, he was a fast bowler and the club's premier batsman. Now he is a medium-paced trundler and an erratic batsman. When he runs in to bowl, he struggles to make it as far as the stumps. He pitches in the perfect spot, just full of a good length, from which a competent batsman can hit the ball effortlessly back over the bowler's head, depositing it among the heifers beyond the boundary.

As a batsman, he has always relied heavily on a good eye. He plays pretty straight, but with the bat well away from the body. He is an old-fashioned cricketer who believes that the ball is there to be hit, and he has the kind of uncomplicated style that must have been used by the game's early practitioners. Perhaps, like them, he believes that LBW is a shameful way to lose your wicket. For in a career stretching back to the early fifties, he has never, ever been out LBW. Not once.

On the other hand, he has lost count of the number of times he has been Run Out. His speciality is to play an aggressive shot off the front foot and to run hell for leather before he has completed the stroke. So he is halfway down the pitch before his partner, backing up with the tortoise-like reactions that are the norm in village cricket, has woken up to what is happening. Whether he has run himself out more times than he has run his partner out is a moot point. Who can say? Only an arithmetical genius. But, seeing as he is a generous cricketer who is always ready to share the pleasure he gets from the game, the odds are that he has been as unstinting in his efforts to run other people out as he has in running himself out. When he trudges back to the pavilion, red-faced and out of breath, it is often the beginning of the end. Invariably his dismissal triggers the lower middle order collapse that is one of the most reliable features of our game.

Now and again, this batsman likes to vary his method of dismissal. If there is a solitary fielder posted out on the boundary, say at deep midwicket or long on, he can pick this player out with amazing accuracy. With every other part of the boundary unguarded and providing a much easier target, this takes a lot of skill.

Another of our batsmen has taken it upon himself to carry out a thorough examination of the umpire's knowledge of the LWB law. A pretty hazardous undertaking, you might think, given that the average village umpire knows as much about the LBW law as he knows about nuclear physics. But this player enjoys a challenge. He enjoys taking risks. So he has perfected a style of play which allows him to get pad on ball, not bat on ball. If there is any way in which the ball can be induced to make contact not with the bat but with the pad, then he can be relied upon to find it. For most batsmen, coordination between hand and eye is crucial; for this guy, it is coordination between leg and eye that is all-important.

Whether he plays forward or back, on the off side or the on, aggressively or defensively, it is the leg that matters. Is it in line with the ball? Is the head over the leg? Is the leg bent or straight? Does he bring the leg straight down the pitch towards the ball? Does he jolt the leg at the moment of impact, getting extra leverage on the ball? Is there a full follow-through?

Another player has developed a unique batting technique. He is a defensive batsman who sells his wicket dearly. However innocuous the bowling, every innings he plays is a battle against the rising ball. Now and again, he gets the ball in the middle of the bat; more often, it comes either off the edge of the bat or off his hands. He is rarely bowled. Edged catches to the close fielders are his particular speciality; his way of solving this problem is to drop the bat at the moment of impact like a plate of hot cakes. His theory is that the gravitational force of a dropped bat takes the sting out of a rising ball and, other things being equal, propels it downwards towards the ground. It is a fine theory. Now and again, once or twice a season perhaps, it seems to work; more often, the bat misses the ball entirely. If the ball is off the wicket, no harm is done – unless he is back on his stumps, playing off the back foot. In that case, the bat can clatter into the base of the stumps. It is surprising that this happens no more than once or twice a season.

What gets another of our players out has nothing to do with the laws of cricket. It is all in the mind. He approaches each innings as if he has been asked to step into the ring with Lennox Lewis. Making his way out to the middle at the start of his innings is an expedition into enemy territory. With a heavy-weight bat and a floppy hat that is much too large for him, he puts me in mind of a colonial soldier with rifle and topi, setting out into the jungle to put down the natives. When he reaches the wicket, he looks around apprehensively. At the crease he is all nerves and fidgets until he has got off the mark. Most batsmen feel the odd butterfly in the stomach as they go out to bat, and only really get rid of it when they get off the mark. Unfortunately, this chap rarely does get off the mark, and so his entire innings is a bundle of nerves. In village cricket the nervous nineties are no problem at all. It is the nervous noughts that are the real bugbear.

*   *   *

How, then, do I get out? Or, to put the question more accurately, how do I get myself out? Like many of our club's batsmen, I receive a high proportion of unplayable deliveries. Invariably, the one that gets me out would have troubled Sachin Tendulkar. When a peach of a ball pitches on the off stump and moves away off the seam, the average village batsman is not good enough to get bat on ball. I may not be good enough to play anything resembling a decent shot, but I am often good enough to get an outside edge onto the ball as it goes through to the keeper. And how many players have the skill to do that? I am also pretty good at dealing with deliveries down the leg side. The leg glance is a favourite shot. Timing is everything. Not many of our players are able to move sufficiently to the off to get inside the line of the ball and then let the ball kiss the face of the bat as it goes through to the keeper. Why did Ranjitsinghi never have this trouble with his leg glance?

I have another, even easier way of getting out, a method beloved by generation upon generation of cricketers: the ball that is just begging to be hit for six. Let's imagine I have hit a nice cover drive, off the meat of the bat, to the short boundary between our two oak trees. When I am in form, I manage to do this at least once a season. But the satisfaction of a perfectly timed shot goes to my head. I am not used to it. So when the next, innocuous delivery comes down, a harmless short-pitched ball just outside the leg stump, I make amends. I give the ball a terrific smash in the direction of the square leg boundary. Late on the stroke and failing to get in line, I succeed only in getting a top edge. I watch as the ball goes spiralling in a gentle arc to mid-on. The fielder there may be in his dotage, but he barely needs to move. It is the dolliest of dolly catches, and he smiles as he clutches the ball to his chest.

Alternatively, the ball begging to be hit for six may be a slow full toss. Unable to believe my luck, I open my shoulders for an unscientific hoick towards cow corner. When I unaccountably fail to make contact, it is a toss up between plumb LBW and a rearranged middle stump.

*   *   *

Any cricketer can make a duck. Especially a village cricketer. But there are ducks and ducks. Our club cherishes, above all, its golden ducks. Every season those who perish first ball are honoured, their names added to the long list of players who have given the club such distinguished service. The achievement is commemorated on a piece of Chiltern beechwood – a rough chunk of wood, shaped like a bat, with a large hole in the middle. We began at the top of the bat, writing each player's name in bold letters, and worked our way down. After a year or two we reached the bottom and repeated the process on the back of the bat. Year after year new names were added and they soon covered both sides of the bat. Then we put it on display behind the pavilion bar, and began again with a new piece of beechwood. And again. A glance down this list of heroes, our golden ducks, is a poignant remembrance of past games and former players. What is especially pleasing is to see there, among the no-hopers and those who rarely troubled the scorers, the names of our star batsmen, those who were always at the top of the averages. It is a nice reminder, like Don Bradman's last Test innings at the Oval, that all cricketers are fallible.

Even a duck can be made with style. On one occasion, Neville Cardus saw his hero, Lancashire's Archie MacClaren,

dismissed without a run to his name. He made what Cardus described as the most immaculate of ducks. The truth is that there is not much style about a nick to the keeper or an LBW decision. Much better, if you have to go, to go with a flourish, middle stump sent cartwheeling out of the ground and bails catapulted almost to the boundary. This is the best way to get out; ask any village batsman. But, as he ruefully stomps off the field back into the pavilion, wait a few minutes before you ask him.

*   *   *

So there are many ways in which a batsman can get himself out. Many of these derive from his technical flaws, but there are others that depend more than anything on human fallibility. A batsman without the mental toughness that all village cricketers need can be sledged out. If he is resilient enough to withstand the sledging, he can be bamboozled out – tricked by a piece of skulduggery. W.G. Grace led the way in 1882, when he ran out the Australian, Sammy Jones, who (believing the ball was dead) left his crease to pat down a divot. That incident so incensed Spofforth, the "demon" bowler, that he took 14 wickets in the match and bowled Australia to victory by seven runs – exactly the same margin of victory achieved by Australia in the 1987 World Cup Final, when Mike Gatting gave such a memorable demonstration of the reverse sweep. We know just how he must have felt. Committing suicide is a method of dismissal village batsmen know all about.

But there is another way of getting out, perhaps the most common of all in village cricket, against which any batsman, however brilliant and however astute he may be, is helpless. It is a method of dismissal that has been relished by generation after generation of cricketers – at least, when the opposition are batting. It may not feature in the laws of the game, but anyone who has ever played cricket knows what it feels like. Being umpired out is an integral part of the village game.

Chapter 9

Accidents will Happen

What Eddie the Eagle was to ski-ing, he is to cricket. Like a heat-seeking missile that destroys itself on impact, he homes in on any potential danger. At an early age he found his niche in the team and made it his own.

When it comes to accidents and injuries, he is in a class of his own. Time and time again he has proved that the simple act of chasing after the ball, picking it up and throwing it in to the keeper isn't simple at all. All kinds of things can happen. A fielder hell-bent on chasing the ball can inadvertently tread on it. The result may be a sprained ankle, a twisted knee or even a bruised coccyx. As he stops and picks up the ball, he can dislocate a finger or graze an elbow. And as he throws the ball in to the keeper, it is the easiest thing in the world to strain a shoulder. If my friend manages to avoid all these hazards, there is every likelihood that he will stub a toe or trip over his own feet.

When the outfield is a mixture of undulating slopes, long grass and rabbit-holes, he is in his element: the potential for accidents and injuries is limitless. But he is capable of making even a perfectly flat outfield seem more like a minefield. He believes that, in the field, speed is everything. His theory is that the faster you run, the easier it is to navigate the boundary. This is an interesting and highly original theory, but its practicality is debatable when his ability to judge either speed or distance is lamentable. His technique may have some merit when he is trying to stop the ball before it reaches a boundary marked by a white line, a rope or a row of flags. But when the boundary is marked by, say, a hedge or a stream (as it is on one or two of the grounds we play on), it can produce interesting results. And when the boundary takes the form of a wooden fence or a brick

wall, the theory is easily demolished – just like the fielder. A
team we once played had their ground adjacent to a field full of
cows. Only when it was too late did my friend realise that our
hosts had taken sturdy precautions to make sure that the cows
could not get into the cricket field. I can see him now, crashing
into a barbed wire fence with all the delicacy of a rhinoceros.

My friend's flair for accidents and injuries is not limited to
the cricket field. Some years ago, when we were on tour, I gave
him a lift in my car. It was a 2CV, a car without frills. Forget
about electrically operated windows: this car did not even have
a mechanical winder to open and close the windows. Just a
simple flap, opened and closed manually. To open the window,
the holding catch was released, and the flap was swung
outwards and up, to be held in place by another catch fixing it to
the upper part of the window. The window was closed by
releasing this catch, whereupon the flap swung down and
slammed shut. We were leaving our pub headquarters on our

way to the match when it happened. The car park was jam-packed, and it took me some time and several three-point turns to edge my way out. My passenger kept himself occupied investigating the mechanism for opening and closing the window. He released the retention catch and swung the flap up. After a bit of a struggle he managed to locate the holding catch at the top and to clip the opened window into place. As I inched my way out of the car park, he decided to close the window. With his right hand, he released the holding catch, allowing the flap to swing down. It slammed down, gathering momentum under its own weight, and crushed the fingers of his left hand, which he had inadvertently left on the sill of the window.

When his bruised knuckles swelled up they looked as if they belonged to a prize fighter who had thrown a lot of punches. But every cloud has a silver lining: with our complement of fit players reduced from twelve to eleven, there was no debate about who to leave out. Single-handedly, he had solved our selection problems.

*   *   *

In village cricket, catches can be a great source of entertainment. Most village cricketers have an extensive repertoire, from those that are too hot to handle to those that are so easy that it is beneath the fielder's dignity even to try. It is surprising how often catches fall invitingly between two fielders, allowing both of them ample time to get to the ball before it reaches the ground. The standard procedure is for each fielder politely to leave it to the other, as much as to say "after you" and "no, I insist, after you." Often this gentlemanly display of good manners is still being played out when the ball plummets to the ground. At the opposite end of the entertainment spectrum are the two fielders who, neither having called "mine," make a simultaneous lunge towards the ball and crash into one another like cars in a head-on collision. A variant of this is when two fielders shout "mine" simultaneously – and crash into one another like cars in a head-on collision.

Throwing the ball in to the keeper can also be an entertaining spectacle. The player who fields the ball may easily strain

his shoulder or pull a muscle; and an unwary fielder can be caught inadvertently in the line of fire, his backside mistaken for the wicket. A misdirected throw can go anywhere. Or, the fielder may fail to release the ball at the right moment: instead of hurtling towards the wicket, it lobs gently up into the air, more like a blow-bubble than a cricket ball. It may even land, embarrassingly, on the fielder's head. Or, the fielder may make a frantic, headlong dive for the ball and just manage to stop it going over the boundary. When he gets to his feet, ball in hand, he can be so dizzy and disorientated that, instead of hurling the ball in to the keeper, he hurls it over the boundary. I have seen it happen.

When the ball is thrown in to the non-striker's end, any fielder who is backing up, hoping to assist in a run out or to prevent overthrows, is liable to get the odd bruise. If he can't get his hands to the ball, he can often get his body in the way. One of our players used to go a stage further. His standard technique for stopping the ball was to use his body rather than his hands. He was a bowler, and if the ball was hit into the outfield, he used to get into position in the approved manner behind the non-striker's wicket, ready to receive the ball if it was thrown to that end. With hands either behind his back or on his knees, he puffed out his chest and made sure it was in line with the throw. When the ball arrived, instead of catching it, he chested it down. Most village cricketers who use their hands when backing up are just as likely to miss the ball as to catch it, and his use of the chest was probably a more effective method of stopping the ball. Unfortunately, his success with this idiosyncratic technique convinced him that he could use the same method to run out the batsman. In game after game, he tried to chest the ball down onto the stumps, determined to prove his point. He was still trying to prove it years later when he retired from the game.

Long ago, when I was a young man, I used to enjoy fielding suicidally close to the bat. I fancied myself as the team's Brian Close, though the only thing we had in common was a lack of hair. I would field either at forward short-leg or silly mid-off. These positions require special qualities in a fielder: reactions like greased lightning, combined with either fearlessness or a high degree of stupidity. When the ball comes straight at you off the meat of the bat, only a fielder with the quickest reactions can get out of the way in time. I was a specialist fielder: what I specialised in were bruised shin-bones and torn finger-nails. Eventually it became clear that my razor-sharp reactions were more suited to a position out in the deep, or – even better – beyond the boundary.

* * *

Nowadays it is not difficult, if you want to go to the seaside for a swim, to find out how polluted or how safe the beach is. Perhaps the cricket authorities should follow suit. Some village grounds could do with danger warnings and safety ratings. The common where one of our local rivals play their cricket has a road running along two sides of it, and when a match is played, the road serves as the boundary. It is not a main road but neither is it a country lane, and every few minutes a car or a van passes by. Most of them travel at a moderate speed, and from time to time someone pulls up and spends a few minutes watching the cricket. Now and again, however, a loud sports car careers down the road with its driver giving a passable imitation of Michael Schumacher. A fielder near the boundary needs to have his wits about him and to keep an eye out for the traffic.

From time to time, a player who is trying to stop the ball going over the boundary or to get under a skier dashes out onto the road in front of an oncoming vehicle. If he is lucky, the driver slams on the brakes in the nick of time. Given the predilection that many cricketers have for statistics, it is surprising that there is no roll of honour in the pavilion to record the names of those players who, over the years, have failed to beat the traffic. Perhaps the Department of Transport should design a new road sign, warning drivers of a cricket hazard: a set of dishevelled stumps, the bails in mid-air, would do nicely. On reflection, two of the existing roads signs would serve equally well: children at play; and senior citizens with walking sticks. Difficult to know which is more appropriate.

*   *   *

Many of our team suffer from nothing more than being overweight and the stiffness that comes with old age. But, we have a small band of players who could fill a casualty ward without looking out of place. There is our opening fast (at least, according to him) bowler, with his permanently injured shoulder, a legacy from the days when he played American football. He can bowl, but he can no longer throw. When he fields the ball, his return to the keeper is as bullet-like as a wet sponge. Then we have our all-rounder with his cartilage trouble; two bowlers with dodgy knees; and finally, a lower order batsman whose faulty forward defensive technique, practised assiduously over many years, has resulted in a bad case of varicose veins.

If there is one part of a cricketer's body that suffers from injury more than any other, it is the back. That, at least, is the experience at our club. Our wicket-keeper's normal pre-match routine is to stretch out flat on his back on the dressing room bench and to close his eyes. In this position he might easily be taken for a corpse – an impression his performance behind the stumps does little to diminish. In fact, with our team of comatose players, a totally stiff fielder would fit in pretty well.

*   *   *

When it comes to injuries, I am not in the same league as my accident-prone friend. But I have chalked up a few successes. Perhaps the most eye-catching was a dislocated little finger. I was fielding at mid-on when I flung myself to the ground, trying to stop a good-looking drive. The ball beat me and went merrily on its way to the boundary. As I hit the deck, arm outstretched, the little finger of my right hand jammed against the ground. While midwicket trotted off to retrieve the ball, I got to my feet and inspected the damage. The finger had a distinctive appearance. From the knuckle joint, it shot out sharply at right angles, as if wanting to get away from the other digits. It was grotesque but, judging by the smiles on the faces of my team-mates, very comical.

Volunteers for anything are usually hard to come by at our club, but there was no shortage of offers to yank the offending finger back into place. After careful consideration (it took me at least half a second), I decided that my little finger would be better off without the tender loving care of my team-mates. As it turned out, my reception in the Accident and Emergency Department of the local hospital was little better. The need for urgent treatment should have been obvious. After all, it was a serious injury – to my dignity, if to nothing else. Inexplicably, a cricketer with a dislocated little finger sticking up into the air at an odd and amusing angle was not seen as the Department's highest priority. Still, it was good to see that, despite all the problems of the health service, the nurses had not lost their sense of humour. They giggled as they went about their work attending to the real emergencies, with only an occasional glance in the direction of my sticking-out little finger. I still don't know what the joke was.

On another occasion, I was fielding at silly mid-on when a batsman stepped out of his crease and crashed the ball straight at me. It came like a bullet, right off the meat of the bat. Not only too fast to get my hands to, but – more to the point – too fast for me to get out of the way. It hit me in the forehead, dead centre between the eyes, and I slumped to the ground. After a moment or two, I staggered to my feet. I was a bit dazed, rather like a boxer who has been knocked down. My team-mates were as generous as ever with their sympathy: "Why didn't you catch the bloody thing? If you'd got your hands to it, it wouldn't have hurt you."

It is surprising how much blood can gush out of a small wound to the forehead. As I was driven away to the hospital, I imagined myself returning to the cricket field like a wounded war hero with a huge bandage across my head. The reality was that when I went back, a couple of hours later, all I had to show for it was two tiny stitches and a half-inch strip of transparent sticking plaster. When our skipper welcomed me back, he was his usual compassionate self: "I knew it looked a lot worse than it was."

During my first season with the club there was one game when, with our regular keeper injured, the skipper asked for a volunteer to keep wicket. I had not been with the club long enough to understand the importance of not volunteering for anything. Surprisingly enough, my performance behind the stumps was remembered not for the number of byes conceded; nor for the dropped catches or the missed stumpings. It was not that there weren't any of these; far from it. It was just that they were overshadowed by something altogether more unusual.

This is what happened. A middle order batsman, who had been at the crease for some time, was playing ball after ball defensively back to the bowler. Suddenly he hit the ball into the gap between mid-on and midwicket, and set off for a single. The fielder at mid-on, seeing the possibility of a run-out, was quick to get to the ball, but he spoiled things by taking his eye off it at the critical moment. He fumbled the ball, and by the time he had it in his hand, the non-striker had had time to complete the run. Nevertheless, the fielder – trying to make up for his misfield – hurled the ball in with all the force he could muster. I had got up to the wicket in the approved manner and, with gloves just above and behind the stumps, I was in a perfect position to take the ball. But instead of thudding into my gloves, it crashed into the stumps. The bails flew up into my face and shattered my spectacles.

There was a delay of several minutes while the umpires inspected the ball and then the pitch to see if there were any tiny fragments of glass there. Finally, they examined my face. For players and spectators alike, this provided an entertaining interlude. It must have made a pleasant change from the tedium of watching a batsman with the attacking instincts of a dormouse.

Cricket fields are often a refuge for birds, and fatalities from the direct blow of a cricket ball are by no means uncommon. But the boot was on the other foot a few seasons ago, when a batsman from Trimdon Colliery in Durham had the ball diverted onto his stumps by a swallow. Personally, I wouldn't

want to get on the wrong side of the red kite we have recently
spotted at several village grounds in the Chilterns; my batting
average is bad enough as it is.

*   *   *

If fielding is a risky business, batting can be positively dangerous. Even running between the wickets is not without its risks.
A batsman diving headlong into the stumps as he tries to avoid
being run out does not usually come to any serious harm, but a
batsman or fielder who finds himself having to vault over the
wicket in an effort to avoid a collision can cause irreparable
damage where he least wants it. Especially if he has left his box
in the pavilion.

Even fatalities to batsmen are not unknown. In 1870, the
Notts player George Summers was fatally hit by the ball while
batting at Lord's against the MCC bowler Platts. With village
pitches not noted for their predictable bounce, it is surprising
there are not more serious injuries. Yet I have seen nothing
worse than pulled muscles, split lips, broken teeth, twisted
knees, torn ligaments, broken fingers, black eyes, bruised
shins, split finger-nails, dislocated shoulders, broken jaws,
cracked ribs, and fractured toes. No serious injuries at all.

Once or twice a season, perhaps, a batsman fails to get out of
the way of the ball, and is carted off to the local hospital for
running repairs. The last time this happened, one of our players
ducked into a rising ball which gave him a nasty cut on his
upper lip. This chap has a loud mouth and is always quick to
give anyone who makes a mistake in the field an earful of
unwanted advice, especially when he is bowling. It was obvious that his lip would need a few stitches. As he was driven off
to hospital, someone found just the right words to send him on
his way: "Let's hope they stitch the top lip to the bottom one".

Chapter 10

Another Language

Googly, yorker, chinaman; long leg, slip, silly point. How can a game that uses words like these be taken seriously?

Googly is a lovely, silly word. Simple to define – an off-break ball bowled with a leg-break action – but not so simple to spot when you are at the crease. The batsman is expecting the ball to turn away from the bat: but it doesn't, it goes the other way. A piece of trickery, a con.

It's not often that a village batsman has to face a leg-break bowler. Shane Warne may have brought it back into the limelight, but its practitioners are still an endangered species. If leg-break bowlers are rare, what is rarer still in village cricket is to come up against a leg-break bowler who can bowl anything like a decent line and length. Any batsman with a bit of patience can count on a couple of free hits an over – a juicy full toss outside the leg stump, say, or a long hop that bounces halfway down the pitch. But patience is not the strongest quality of the average village batsmen. So any leg-spinner, however hopeless, is sure to pick up a few wickets.

When the leg-spinner gets it right, the batsman is pretty clueless. The approved, orthodox way of dealing with a leg spinner is to play with the spin, hitting the ball through the off side. But the logic behind this is far too complex for the village cricketer. Much simpler to stick to the tried and trusted way of dealing with any bowler who gives the ball a bit of air – an agricultural heave across the line towards cow corner. There is a fifty-fifty chance of connecting; and if the batsman misses the ball entirely, there is a pretty good chance that it will miss the stumps. A wild swing need not be suicidal – at least, not always.

If the leg-spinner who can bowl a decent line and length is rare, the leg-spinner who can bowl a decent googly is rarer still. Most village batsmen have one way of dealing with a bowler who delivers the ball off a run-up of one yard and tosses it high into the air. He is like a red rag to a bull. The batsman goes down the pitch to him. If he gets to the ball before it pitches, it won't matter whether it's a leg-break or a googly.

If he doesn't get bat on ball until after it has pitched, the batsman's stroke will be the same regardless of what type of ball it is. He will still give it an almighty thump and try to put it into the next field – without having the faintest idea whether it's a leg-break, a googly, or even a top spinner. After it leaves the bat, its path may well be vertical rather than horizontal. Where it will end up is anyone's guess.

So, the googly is wasted. When the batsman plays the same stroke regardless of which way the ball is turning – because he hasn't the faintest idea which way it is turning – a delivery that does the opposite of what is expected is too clever by half. The googly is just too sophisticated for village cricket. But still, a lovely word.

The yorker has an interesting derivation. "To put Yorkshire on someone" was an old dialect expression meaning to cheat or trick. Once again, cricket and skulduggery are not far apart. As with the googly, the success of the yorker depends entirely on deceit. But there is one crucial difference. To bowl a yorker, a bowler needs some help from the batsman. Any well-pitched-up ball on the stumps can be turned into a yorker, and many village batsmen are happy to oblige. Usually the victim is looking to play an attacking shot to a ball that he mistakes for a full toss or a half-volley. But before he can get the bat down, the ball passes underneath it and crashes into the stumps.

It's not easy for a village batsman to keep a yorker out. The trouble is that he has to forget his attacking instincts, keep the bottom of his bat in contact with the ground, and concentrate on keeping the ball out. This, of course, is anathema to most village batsmen, who believe that attack is the best form of defence. A batsman who attacks the bowling is always popular with the spectators – and with any opposition bowler who can produce a decent yorker.

If the batsman struggles against the googly and the yorker, what chance does he have against the chinaman? No wonder he is confused. Experts cannot even agree on a definition. Is it the left-arm wrist-spinner's equivalent of the googly; or is it his stock ball, breaking from off to leg when bowled to a right-handed batsman – in other words, the precise opposite? Either way, it hardly matters. As with the googly, the difference is academic. His chances of making contact with the ball are just the same.

* * *

Silly words. But those describing some of the fielding positions are even sillier. Take long leg. I first heard it as a boy in the early fifties. I was listening, with my cricket-mad uncle and grandfather, to the radio commentary of a Test Match against the Australians, with Hutton and Compton batting. I imagined a fielder with abnormally long legs: a fielder on stilts, a human daddy-long-legs. In the same Test Match, the commentator said that Neil Harvey was fielding "in the covers." I pictured a huge cowshed along one side of the ground, with a roof stretching out over the cricket field and "covering" the deep fielders.

The spot where long leg stands at one end of our ground is in front of the pavilion. This is handy if the fielder needs to pop into the pavilion between overs to attend to a call of nature, and when the tea interval comes, he can be off the field first. But proximity to the pavilion is not such an advantage when he has to deal with a ball heading for the boundary – and the opposition's batsmen, waiting to go in, are watching like vultures, willing the ball to go over the line. The fielder just knows that they want him to make a mess of it. Having to perform in front of a hostile gallery does not help his concentration and so, more often than not, he does not disappoint them.

"Slip: to make a careless or casual mistake." That is the dictionary definition. So, the word is perfectly suited to a fielding position where the tiniest mistake can change the whole course of the game. If catches win matches, slip catches win more than most. More to the point, they also lose more than most. There are just so many ways in which a slip fielder can foul up. As the bowler runs in to bowl, he can agonise over whether to watch the ball or the edge of the bat, and end up doing neither. One of our players has solved this quandary to his own satisfaction, if not to anyone else's, by watching the edge of the ball.

The slip fielder can take off just a fraction too late to stop a high ball going over his head, and see it go sailing to the boundary. He can fling himself to the ground just too late to prevent the ball going underneath him. He can dive forward and catch the ball on the half-volley just an instant after it has touched the ground. Now and again he can even make a blinding catch, spoiled only when his elbow jars against the ground as he comes to earth and sends the ball spiralling out of his hand. He can leave the catch to the keeper, and then watch as the keeper leaves it to him and the ball shoots off towards the boundary.

Slip is a specialist position – a position for the senior professional whose approach to fielding is based on old-fashioned manners and letting others go first. So he leaves any sharp chances to someone else, and if the ball goes past him he allows one of the other slips to chase it, while he looks on giving lots of moral support but no actual help. One team we used to play against always had the same man at first slip, a tall, good-natured chap with long arms and safe hands. He stayed there throughout the innings, whether the bowling was fast or slow, seam or spin. He was there year after year, the same man in precisely the same position. If the ball went past him, he never gave chase. He just stood there and watched while someone else went after the ball. One day a misdirected drive flew off the edge of the bat and hit him just below the knee. It was a fearful blow, but instead of the crack of ball on shin-bone, there was an awful hollowness about the sound. As the ball rebounded and went out towards point, the fielder, unhurt and unconcerned, made a minor adjustment to his artificial leg.

The slip fielder is ideally placed to combine minimum exer-

tion with maximum conviviality. If he is lucky, he can spend the entire game doing nothing more than walk, at the end of every over, from one end of the pitch to the other. He can concentrate on what he does best – chatting to the keeper and giving a batsman who is just about to play the ball the occasional, well-timed word of advice.

Silly point, like silly mid-on and silly mid-off, is a very silly position. The fielder is too close to the bat to have any realistic chance of taking a catch. At least, he would be too close if he stayed where he had been put. But in village cricket, the skipper's direction to field in such-and-such a position is little more than a basis for negotiation. Any experienced player who is asked to field in a suicidal position knows how to deal with the situation. It is not long before he makes an appropriate adjustment. Of course, he does not make this too obvious. For the first few deliveries he may even stay within a few feet of the position he should be in. But the end of an over provides an ideal opportunity to put things right. When he returns to that position, only the sharpest of skippers will notice that he is a good deal deeper than he should be. If the skipper does notice, he can take an ostentatious stride towards the wicket and still be a good two yards further out than his original position. What is the use of playing cricket year after year if you don't learn a thing or two?

*   *   *

If cricket has silly words for different deliveries and different fielding positions, it has lovely words to describe the different ways in which a batsman can put bat on ball. My favourite shot is a delicate little cut which, properly timed when there is a fast outfield and no third man, produces four easy runs. The shot can be played with minimal foot movement and little or no back-lift. I don't know why, but my team-mates insist that this shot is not a cut, but a dab. Perhaps the dictionary definition provides a clue: "dab: to aim a feeble blow".

Dab is not a bad word, but there are plenty of better ones to describe how the bat can make contact with ball. A batsman bent on aggression can bang, bash, crack, crash, clump, clobber, thump, thrash, thwack, smack, swot, whack or wallop the ball. If he puts bat to ball in a slightly more scientific way, he can drive, drill, hammer, whip, rifle or chop. And if, contrary to the instincts of most village batsmen, he prefers guile to brute force, he can push, paddle, glance, stroke, steer, squeeze, nudge or even nurdle the ball.

Cricket needs its vocabulary; it needs to be written about. The more words, the more newspaper articles, the better. When the match reports have been read, the words can be put to good use. Many cricket grounds are notorious for the hardness of their seats, and a carefully folded newspaper placed between bottom and seat enables you to watch the game in comfort, consoled by the solace of good writing. Watching cricket has been compared to reading poetry. If you have played cricket on a damp Saturday in September, on an exposed ground high up in the Chilterns, on a square where the direction of the ball after pitching is as predictable as the English weather, you will know what a poetic game cricket can be.

Chapter 11

Googlies

The googly is not what it seems. Its purpose is to deceive and trick the batsman. So it has become a metaphor for anything artful: the kind of con you expect from a card-sharp or a conjurer.

Or a cricketer. To the casual observer, cricket seems a quiet, peaceful game, with nothing much going on. Men in white dotted across a green field: a batsman not in a hurry, a bowler running in mechanically, and fielders without much energy or interest. But, as with the googly, things are not always what they seem. The comatose batsman might be conning the opposition: lulling them into a false sense of security, trying to convince them that he is a plodder who cannot hit the ball off the square. Then, when the fielders have been brought in around the bat, he can launch himself into his favourite heave to cow-corner.

And the bowler's succession of tired, innocuous deliveries, his arm getting lower and lower, may also be a con: a cunning plan to make the batsman relax before surprising him with a good length ball that pitches on the off stump and moves away just enough to find the outside edge.

The fielders too may be playing the same game. Cover point can drift far enough out to give the batsman a single. He can run after the ball like an old woman, and throw it in to the keeper like a soft marshmallow. But who knows? It may be an act. This incompetent may suddenly transform himself into an ace fielder. Having conned the batsman into taking one single too many, he may pounce and hurl the ball in like a bullet, shattering the stumps with the batsman well short of the crease.

Or not. Is it bluff, or double bluff? Perhaps he really is as hopeless as he seems. Perhaps he only wants to make the opposition **think** he is a cunning devil, a cricketer who cannot possibly be as incompetent as he seems. If his opponent is expecting the unexpected, he may not be prepared when the unexpected does not come. Double bluff. Clever stuff – if the player who tries it doesn't end up more confused than the player he is trying to con.

The rainy weather that coincides, year-in year-out, with the start of the cricket season is another kind of googly. The pattern is always the same. A fortnight before the season begins there is brilliant spring sunshine. The players rummage around for their cricket gear, scrape last September's mud off their boots, and dream of summer. Then, on the first Saturday of the season, the weather changes. Overnight a depression has moved in from the Atlantic. It reaches England around mid-day, and stays there.

By the time the two teams arrive at the ground, the pitch has been transformed into a duck-pond. With the rain lashing down without let-up all afternoon, and the game abandoned without a ball being bowled, a player who arrives home just as the pubs are closing needs to have his wits about him. Oddly enough, a partner prepared to put up with an afternoon's absence to play cricket is not necessarily prepared to put up with an afternoon spent propping up the bar. But, if the history of cricket proves anything, it is that gambling and drinking have always been as much a part of the game as anything that goes on on the field of play. So a player can convince himself that the distinction is academic, and say with a perfectly clear conscience that he has spent the afternoon "at the cricket".

During an average summer, the weather presents the skipper of the home team with another googly approximately every other week: when and whether to call the game off. How he handles it depends on whether he is an optimist or a pessimist.

The optimist delays a decision until the last possible moment, hoping against hope that – despite all evidence to the contrary – the rain will miraculously stop and the sun will suddenly appear and beat down from a cloudless sky. It is only when 22 players have turned up at the ground that he goes out to the middle, discovers a strip that looks more like a paddy field than a cricket pitch, and calls the game off. That is when the players curse the skipper for ruining their afternoon by not calling the game off sooner.

The pessimist spots a couple of dark clouds on the horizon, tunes in to a weather forecast predicting rain, and calls the game off before most of the players have got out of bed. It is only at two o'clock, when the sun is beating down out of a cloudless sky and instead of playing cricket most of the players are DIYing or digging their gardens, that they curse the skipper for ruining their afternoon.

*   *   *

A googly of a different sort faces the fixture secretary when he has to drop a long-established fixture. There can be many reasons for dropping a team from the club's fixture list. Teams change over the years; the opposition may be weaker than they were, unable to give us a decent game: it's possible, just. More probably, they are stronger than they were, and we are unable to give them a decent game.

There are other, more serious reasons for dropping a fixture. A club that plays its home fixtures on a Council recreation ground, where the upkeep of the ground is entrusted to the same department that maintains the municipal refuse tip. Or, a cricket tea that just does not measure up to the standards any village team has a right to expect. Or, worst of all, a failure to uphold the spirit as well as the laws of the game: when the opposition takes off after the match without so much as a glance towards the bar. Then there are no two ways about it: the time has come to pull the plug.

So. The decision has been taken. The team in question is history. All the fixture secretary has to do is to break the news. Another googly to be negotiated. There are plenty of options: he can dream up a wedding that will prevent his club from putting out a team on the day in question. But for any club that takes its cricket at all seriously, this sounds pretty lame. The fixture secretary may prefer something a little more elaborate, such as a special match against the president's eleven. It may be that this fictitious match just has to be played on the date previously assigned to the club you want to drop. Or, if you want to be little more subtle, it may have had a knock-on effect, resulting in a wholesale restructuring of the fixture list and the regrettable but unavoidable loss of some long-standing fixtures.

If the fixture secretary wants something a bit simpler, he can always claim to have made a mistake over dates. When you have been playing the same team on exactly the same date of the cricketing calendar for the past ten years, this may not sound totally convincing. But since all fixture secretaries can be relied upon to get their fixtures in a muddle from time to time, a mix-up over dates can sound totally plausible.

Whichever excuse he uses, he can say how sorry he is and how keen he is to reinstate the fixture at some (unspecified) time in the future. An ability to be economical with the truth is an indispensable qualification for any self-respecting fixture secretary. But if all else fails, there is one other option, so outlandish that it is often overlooked. It goes against the grain, but desperate situations sometimes call for desperate remedies: the fixture secretary can always resort to telling the plain, unadulterated truth.

*   *   *

With the opportunity to play cricket limited to just one afternoon a week, it stands to reason that every batsman wants to spend as much time as possible at the crease. So when a wicket falls, the next man in loses no time in getting out to the middle as quickly as he can. Right?

Wrong. Many players are only too happy to spend as much time as they can in the pavilion and as little time as they can on the cricket field. So, as often as not, the incoming batsman is nowhere to be seen. If the skipper is lucky, he may be padded up and skulking in some half-hidden corner of the pavilion. When the skipper spots him and gives him his usual pep talk ("You're in. Get out there and stay there") he emerges onto the field rubbing his eyes like some nocturnal creature unaccustomed to the light of day. If the skipper is not so lucky, the bats-

man who should be on his way out to the middle is asleep
behind the wheel of his car, oblivious to everything and everyone. When roused, he breaks into a mad scramble to get his box,
pads and gloves on. Then he searches frantically for his bat.

It is surprising that more village batsmen are not given out
"timed out". The law allows an incoming batsmen just three
minutes to get himself out to the middle. Perhaps village skippers are sporting souls who prefer to get their opponents out fair
and square in one of the "proper" ways? And perhaps pigs
might fly. Perhaps their grasp of the laws is a bit shaky? More
than likely. Or, perhaps a few extra minutes of enforced idleness are not altogether unwelcome? Now, that's more like it.

If getting the players to go out to the middle to bat is so difficult, what chance is there of getting them to go out to the middle
to drag the plastic sheet over the pitch when rain interrupts
play? Very little. They know that the slower they are to get the
covers (as we like to call our thin sheet of plastic) onto the pitch,
the wetter it will get and the longer it will take to dry out – and
the more time they will be able to spend chatting to their friends
in the pavilion. For most of them, this is infinitely preferable to
running about on a damp cricket field.

The tea interval, too, is usually a languid, long-drawn-out
affair. And when the players have munched their way through
a four-course tea, when they have scoffed the last mouthful and
drained the last cupful, they can be relied upon to use every
trick in the book to put off – for as long as possible – the dreaded
moment when they have to drag themselves out of the pavilion
and onto the field. It is astonishing how, at the very moment
when the skipper wants to lead his men out onto the field, an
entire team can vanish into thin air.

* * *

Which guard to take? Another dilemma, another googly that
faces every village cricketer. Middle is the traditional call,
beloved by those who like to put bat to ball and maintain,
reasonably enough, that putting the bat in the middle of the
stumps gives them the best chance of making contact. Leg is the
stance favoured by those who fancy themselves as styl-

ists ... this is often those with the greatest pretensions and the least ability. Middle and leg is the middle-of-the-road guard – for batsmen who cannot make up their mind whether they want to thump the ball, or place it scientifically into the empty spaces. Often they end up doing neither.

These are the traditional stances, but they are not the only ones. One of our players asks for one leg, and then carefully places the tip of his bat down a couple of inches outside the leg stump. This gives him room to play the ball through the off side with a full flourish of the bat – an excellent strategy if the ball pitches on the wicket. It is not, however, the ideal technique for dealing with a ball that comes into the wicket from outside the leg stump, as a glance at his batting average shows. At the other extreme is our lower order batsman who takes an off stump guard, on the grounds that this allows him to play his favourite shot, an on-drive. When he gets it right, this is indeed a nice shot, executed with the full face of the bat and a beautiful follow-through. And he gets it right at least once a season.

*   *   *

Googlies are everywhere: among the little, everyday conundrums that face anyone who is involved with a village cricket team. For example, if your team has been comprehensively outplayed, the match report for your local newspaper can be a bit tricky. Of course, you could always send in a fair, factual report, recording the grim details with brutal honesty. It can happen. I once came across a report like that. A collector's item.

Most village teams deal with this problem a little differently. It is known as "creative reporting". All that is needed is to exercise a little discretion as to what goes in and what is left out – a little exaggeration here, a little dissimulation there. No barefaced untruths, of course – that's not cricket. Just a bit of judicious editing. It can improve your team's performance out of all recognition.

There is an alternative solution, one that is altogether easier. After all, no one has a perfect memory. Anyone can forget to send in the occasional match report. And if the oversight happens to coincide with your team's most inept performance of the season, that is just a happy coincidence.

* * *

The treasurer of a village cricket club is a very important person. The position calls for a formidable range of skills. Organisational ability and the capacity to make figures add up are the first essentials...or so one would have thought. The truth is, that one of the most successful treasurers our club has ever had was hopeless at figures and could not have organised a bun-fight in a bakery. He was admired for his ability to stuff cheques, IOUs, and bills into his pockets at random; to scribble receipts onto any odd scrap of paper that came to hand; and then to produce a set of figures at the AGM that seemed to make sense. Amazing. But he had what it takes. He knew that the most important aspects of the job had nothing to do with arithmetic and organisation, and everything to do with handling people: brow-beating the players into parting with their subscriptions; sweet-talking the vice-presidents into making a hefty donation to club funds. With the gift of the gab and the skin of a rhinoceros, the job fitted him like a glove.

When it comes to the annual begging letters to the vice presidents, the treasurer needs to tread carefully. The expectation of financial support must be implied rather than spelt out. Most treasurers favour a three-pronged attack. First, they paint a rosy picture of the club's achievements over the past year (if these are non-existent, the treasurer can use his imagination here). Second, they give an upbeat description of the club's ambitions for the next year (this bit is easy: after all, there is all the difference in the world between ambitions and their realisation). Finally, they stress that the club's future well-being depends on the support of its players and of its vice presidents, who have been so generous in the past. This usually does the trick.

If not, the treasurer can send out a second, less subtle letter: the pavilion is badly in need of refurbishment; the club needs a new mower/roller/anything else that comes to mind; and the cricket club must be supported if it is to survive and to continue to play the role it has always played in the life of the community. This can be coupled with a flowery acknowledgement of past support, a fervent request to do the club the great honour of agreeing to serve once again as an honorary vice president, and – the final clincher – the promise that the vice-presidents' names will be printed on the front page of the club's fixture card, complimentary copies of which will be sent to the local newspaper, the parish magazine, and leading lights of the community.

*   *   *

With one or two notable exceptions, most of our team need little persuading to put their hands in their pockets for a round of drinks. Persuading them to part with a slightly larger sum of money for their annual subscription, however, is another matter altogether. It is like getting blood out of a stone. We have tried everything. Our first attempt at solving the problem was to appeal to players' better nature. We should have known better.

Our second brainwave was to offer a discount for early payment. It seemed a good idea at the time. The principle was sound. The only, ultimately insuperable, difficulty was to hit on the right amount. A small discount had no effect whatever, while a large discount had too much effect: with virtually every player quick to take advantage, the result was a serious dent in the club's revenue.

Our third idea was to introduce a penalty for late payment. But this fared no better, and a small penalty had no effect at all. When we substituted a large penalty, this should have solved the problem. But we had reckoned without the guile and ingenuity of experienced professionals. Every excuse under the sun was trotted out. Eventually the committee decided that desperate measures were called for. "If you don't pay, you can't play" became the rule.

After two or three games, it was clear that the new policy was a great success...if we wanted to play every game with eight or nine players. So the committee scratched their heads and thought again. And we reverted to our old, sloppy ways. Our club may not have much money in the bank, but at least we can put out a team of eleven.

How to attract youngsters to the game? A perennial problem for most village clubs. Over the years we have tried everything: word of mouth, advertisements in the local rag, posters stuck up around the village, circulars dropped through letter boxes, approaches to local schools and youth clubs. Everything.

Eventually we realised that we were targetting the wrong kids – kids whose Saturday afternoons were already spoken for, taken up by the kind of activities no modern youngster can afford to miss out on. New fads like skateboarding and computer games; old fads like hanging out on street corners and chasing girls. We recognised the need to get them hooked on the game at a much earlier age. So we racked our brains, thinking of ways in which families with very young children could be encouraged to get involved with the club. We realised that we had to think the unthinkable – to think out of the box. The most imaginative suggestions were vetoed by the committee due to their over-reliance on drinking and gambling – a sad state of affairs when one considers that these are two of the game's oldest traditions. But eventually we hit upon an idea. It was novel and radical, but what the hell. Why not get the kids to play cricket?

And so our club made a foray into the world of kwik cricket, where boys and girls from the age of four learn what it feels like to get bat on the ball – something most of our players have been trying to do, with limited success, for their entire careers. The sight of seventy or eighty kids with plastic bats and balls enjoying themselves hugely is a pretty amazing sight. What is even more amazing is to see a clutch of our players out there, supervising the kids. At least, that's what they say they're there for. What they are really doing, I suspect, is to watch and to learn. If they can pick up a few tips here and there, one or two of them might just get their batting average into double figures.

Chapter 12

Time for Tea

"We are not first class batsmen, but we will give you a good tea. Home made cakes." The secretary of Deopham, a village in Norfolk, had his priorities right when he wrote to confirm a fixture against a visiting team. When it comes to compiling a decent fixture list, there is only one criterion that counts.

Once upon a time, long ago, we played against a club that had an exceptionally attractive ground, with a nice, old-fashioned pub opposite. It was a sunny afternoon and we had a good, close game. There was only one thing missing: a decent tea. In over twenty-five years of village cricket, I have never come across a tea like it. It was a disgrace. In fact, "tea" is a misnomer for what was offered. Not only were there no sandwiches and no cakes – believe it or not, there was no tea: just tepid orange cordial poured into paper cups. The food consisted of crisps, cheeselets, peanuts and other bits and pieces from the local supermarket, picked up on his way to the match by a player whose priorities were speed, cheapness and his own convenience. The club might as well have greeted us with a large placard emblazoned in capital letters: WE DO NOT WISH TO PLAY YOU NEXT YEAR.

When our season is over, the club's stalwarts keep winter at bay for a few more weeks by getting together to mull over the summer's ups and downs. Now and again, the conversation may turn to an exciting game or a memorable innings. But when it comes to raking over the season and deliberating over the merits of different fixtures, there is only one thing that really counts: the quality of the tea.

Sandwiches – proper sandwiches made with fresh crusty bread – are the centre-point of a good cricket tea. The doorsteps of one team we used to play against were filled to bursting with thick slices of home-cured ham; and then there was fresh salad, home-made cakes with cream or jam bulging out of them, and as many mugs of tea as you could drink. The tea was properly brewed, poured from a gigantic teapot and served with fresh milk – not the UHT apology now served up at most county grounds. This was one match for which we never had the slightest difficulty finding players.

These opponents had one player who never bowled and whose top score, judging by his efforts when he came to the wicket as a perpetual number eleven, was nought not out. At first this puzzled us. How could a player like this keep his place in what was otherwise a pretty strong team? After we had been playing them for a few years, with the same chap always coming in at number eleven, the penny dropped. After the game, he was always to be seen having a quiet drink with the same lady – the lady who always prepared the tea. His wife. How could it have taken us so long to work this out? It was the obvious explanation. What better qualification is there be for a village cricket team? With a wife who made the best cricket teas for miles around – a wife who was happy to do teas, week in week out, if her husband was playing – his name must have been the first on the team-sheet.

* * *

When we are in the field first, the tea interval is our oasis. If things are not going too well, it's a long time coming. As soon as the umpires remove the bails and walk off, the fielders have a new spring in their step. All eleven want to be first into the pavilion, and they make a beeline for one of two places – the loo or the tea table.

But which is it to be? Each player has to make a snap decision, and it is a dilemma far more difficult than anything he has had to cope with during the game. With just one WC between twenty-two players, it's an agonising choice – especially on very cold days or on very hot days when there have been frequent drinks intervals. Whether you are first or last in the queue can make all the difference.

Anyone who puts the loo first is taking a big risk when it comes to tea. He will probably have no difficulty getting a cup of tea. If he is lucky, he may even manage to get his hands on a sandwich – albeit one that no one else wants. But his chances of getting anywhere near the pile of home-made cakes before it has been reduced to rubble are less than zero.

The tea interval is an opportunity for the fielding side to rest their sore feet – even if most of them have spent the entire afternoon doing exactly that. For those players whose idea of cricket does not include undue exertion (a category which includes the whole of our team), the half-hour break is the highlight of the game. It is an ideal time for all those activities that are an essential part of cricket but do not involve the inconvenience of having to play. This is when the players can catch up on scurrilous gossip; indulge in character assassinations of their team-mates; inflict unfunny jokes on a captive audience; and, best of all, complain about the skipper and his absurd bowling changes, ridiculous field placings, ludicrous batting order and general all-round incompetence.

For a smoker, the tea interval is even more precious. He may have been able to snatch a puff or two during the game (especially if he has been fielding on the boundary), but village skippers can be surprisingly intolerant. Don't they know that four of the very greatest English batsmen were inveterate smokers? Hobbs, Hammond, Hutton and Compton are not a bad quartet to emulate.

Rest and recuperation may seem to be the order of the day, but the truth is that the tea interval brings out the competitive spirit of the players far more effectively than anything that goes on on the cricket field. In a no-holds-barred tussle across the tea table, it is those who have had the benefit of etiquette training from an early age who come off best. This is where free-for-alls at toddlers' birthday parties prove their worth, as eleven pairs of hands make a simultaneous grab for the chocolate cake. Team spirit is all very well on the cricket field; when it comes to tea, it is every man for himself.

Any player who has not had the advantages of early training

must prepare himself for the fray as best he can. He can begin by boning up on essential interpersonal skills, such as assertiveness and dealing with difficult people; but if he is to make a real impact he will have to learn more robust, physical skills. Like judo and all-in wrestling.

Paradoxically, the more sluggish a player is on the cricket field, the more likely it is that he will move around the tea table like greased lightning. This is where strategic planning comes into its own. Experienced players use a three-fold strategy. First, a birds-eye scan of the tea table, fixing the exact location of the fattest sandwiches and the creamiest cakes. Second, a quick grab for the most favourably positioned chair – the one closest to whichever home-made cake has been cut into the largest portions. And, finally, a single-minded swoop across the table, sweeping up as much grub as can be piled onto a single plate. When every player has the same plan of attack, it takes only a few moments for the tea table to be left looking as if it has been ravaged by a marauding army.

Those whose speed of reaction does not match up to the high standards required, find themselves squeezed out and marginalised. They have to do the best they can from seats near the end of the table. From here a player with longer-than-average arms may be able to purloin the odd sandwich or sausage roll; but he will have his work cut out to get anywhere near the chocolate cake.

Now and again, a newcomer may try a more cultured approach: "would you mind passing down the cake, please?" But with temporary deafness a common affliction around the tea table, its chances of success are pretty slim. When a player is simultaneously slurping tea, arguing with his neighbour and stuffing himself silly, responding to a polite request is not a high priority. Eventually someone may take pity on the unfortunate soul at the end of the table, and pass the plate of cakes down to him. This is usually after the one cake left has been intimately examined and rejected by everyone else.

Like a new boy at school, a new player may need a little time to settle down; it may take him a game or two to get used to the team ethic. But after a couple of matches he will get fed up with spending the tea interval not eating tea, but watching the rest of the team eat tea. He will realise that "learning by doing" is the best way to learn, and his table manners will sink to the necessary level. ˙

*   *   *

Some villages have a competition for the "best kept garden," but there is another -less official, but far more cut-throat – competition: the best cricket tea. The contestants are prepared to go to any lengths to gain an advantage, and they research their market thoroughly, using the most sophisticated modern techniques. Focus groups, often disguised as coffee mornings or jumble sales, are used to gather intelligence and identify players' likes and dislikes. This professionalism makes the players' attempts to outsmart their opponents on the cricket field look decidedly amateurish.

For many years, our club agonised over the issue of league cricket. Many of the villages we had traditionally played against had gone into a local league, and it was becoming increasingly difficult for us to obtain Saturday fixtures. Some members argued that, in addition to ensuring a decent Saturday fixture list, joining the local village league would help to raise playing standards and to attract younger players. Others believed that league cricket would make it difficult for us to accommodate players past their prime – and players who have never had, and will never have, a prime. Since these are just the kind of players who are the backbone of our team, they had a point.

We decided to pilot the idea of league cricket by setting up a virtual league, giving every team we played against a certain number of points and then arranging the teams into a league table. Runs scored and wickets taken would have been the conventional basis for awarding points, but we decided that it would be more in keeping with the game's traditions to base them on something closer to the heart of village cricketers: the tea.

So, compliments and criticisms over the tea table were converted into marks out of ten. Some criteria were established: home-made cakes were a pre-requisite for any score above five; quantity was no less important than quality; and a list of select items was agreed – scones with jam or cream, strawberries, chocolate cake – for the award of bonus points. It was a nice idea, but it did not last long. The league table had been in operation for only three or four weeks when one of our players suggested that the rock cakes provided by one team were more rock than cake. A harmless enough remark – if the baker of the rock cakes had not been within earshot. We soon realised that the awarding of points for cricket teas was a minefield that we would do well to avoid.

* * *

The players, the umpires and the scorers all have tea provided for them. But what about the spectators? Most village clubs give their handful of supporters a free cup of tea and let them polish off the odd sandwich left over when the cricketers have finished. Spectators at our matches are usually outnumbered by the half-dozen heifers in the adjacent field, but it is amazing how their number can swell as the tea interval approaches. One or two of our old boys, however, are not content to rely on the leftovers. They have perfected a technique for sidling up alongside the team without being noticed and unobtrusively spiriting away a sandwich or two. The skipper may roar at his players like a sergeant major, but when it comes to ticking off an old man who has helped himself to a free tea, he is more like the cowardly lion.

However, the most guileful pilferers of cricket teas are not old men, but small boys. Usually they belong to the most obnoxious members of the opposition. Their heads barely reaching the tea table, they can infiltrate a line of cricketers and magic away a handful of crisps before you can say Jack Robinson. One can only admire their dexterity; perhaps they see this as an apprenticeship. Ideal practice, perhaps, for Fagin's gang of pickpockets in the school production of *Oliver*?

*   *   *

In village cricket, the time of the tea interval is agreed by the skippers before play begins. Occasionally, interruptions for rain or the state of the game may persuade them that it would make sense to change the agreed time, and to take tea either earlier or later than planned. This may make sense to the skippers, but it is guaranteed to give the tea-maker apoplexy. To her, the agreed time is sacrosanct, and any attempt to change it is tantamount to the collapse of civilisation as she knows it. To convince her otherwise is beyond the capability of the most persuasive of skippers. It is much easier to stick to the original time, and to move heaven and earth to fit the game in around the tea. Since most players consider the tea far more important than the game, this makes a lot of sense.

Taking tea "between the innings" is a gambit favoured by some opposition skippers. This apparently innocent suggestion is fraught with danger. If you lose the toss and find yourself in the field, you are at the mercy of a skipper whose idea of an enjoyable game is to spend twice as much time batting as field-ing. If, on the other hand, you win the toss, decide to bat, and by some miracle you manage to survive with some wickets in hand until the normal time for tea, you are faced with a difficult dilemma. How on earth can you know when to declare? What-ever time you choose is likely to be wrong. Declare too late, and your bowlers will curse you for not giving them enough time to bowl out the opposition. Declare too early, and your whole team will curse you for losing the match. Much better to stick to a fixed time for tea. After all, one of the most important skills of the leader, as any skipper knows, is the ability to avoid like the plague anything resembling a difficult decision.

* * *

In 1984, David Constant and Alan Whitehead, umpiring in a match between Hampshire and Essex, had their tea taken out to them on the square. In doing this they were following the prece-dent set by the famous Notts player Arthur Shrewsbury, who, batting in the days before the tea interval was introduced into county cricket, always had a cup of tea taken out to him at precisely half past four. Constant and Whitehead were protest-ing against the shortening of the tea interval to just fifteen minutes. In a village match, that is barely enough time for the players to have got through the first joke.

It is a hot afternoon, the opposition have scored 200 runs without losing a wicket, and your bowlers have tried everything they know – and found that the opposition's batsmen know rather more. That is when, on scores of cricket grounds all over England, you can hear the same plaintive cry: "How long is it to tea?"

Chapter 13

"To play Cricket-a-Wicket, and be Merry"

In its early days, cricket was regarded as a worthless pastime, encouraging idleness, drinking and gambling. No wonder the game's popularity soared. "A wet day; only three members present; nine bottles of wine" ran an early entry in the record book of the famous Hambledon club; and the Bat and Ball Inn on Broadhalfpenny Down sold ale that "would flare like turpentine, genuine Boniface, that would put the souls of three butchers into one heaven."

Beer and cricket have always gone together. Cricket was first played in that part of southern England known as the Weald, and it is striking that the best known of the early village clubs – such as Farnham and Sutton in Surrey, and Maidstone and Sevenoaks in Kent – were in districts where the cultivation of hops was a mainstay of the local economy.

George Parr and Julius Caesar were two early cricketers who worked harder than most to maintain the game's links with the brewing industry. Before one important game, however, they agreed to abandon their normal routine and to reduce their consumption by half. Their bodies could not cope with this sudden change in the habits of a lifetime and, far from enhancing their performance, the new regime resulted in a sudden loss of form. So after two days of semi-abstinence they abandoned the experiment and resumed their normal habits. They even went a little further, reasoning that they would stand an even better chance of success if they made up for what they had missed on the two previous days.

"Silver Billy" Beldham, Richard Nyren (secretary and

captain of the Hambledon club) and William Clarke (who was owner of the Trent Bridge Inn in Nottingham) are among early players who combined cricket with careers as pub landlords. Sadly, we have no landlords in our team, but a couple of players who are the sons of publicans do their best to keep up the old standards.

Today, as in the past, village cricket gives the players a wonderful excuse for skiving off work and getting together with their drinking pals on a regular basis. Outside the cricket season, things are not quite so easy. But, with a little ingenuity and some creative thinking, the determined player can find sufficient committee meetings and sub-committee meetings to overcome the difficulty. If he is really desperate, he can even arrange some net practice. Half an hour in the nets followed by a couple of hours in the pub is a pretty good way of keeping in condition during the winter. After all, no one can expect to do himself justice when the cricket season starts unless he has made an effort to keep up to scratch during the winter.

* * *

A team meeting to discuss tactics is an essential part of the team's pre-match preparation. The more discussion there is, the better; a two-hour long meeting in the local pub is ideal. A casual observer could be forgiven for mistaking this for a lunch-time drinking session, but those who do not understand village cricket cannot be expected to appreciate its subtleties. The distinction between tactical discussion and booze-up is very subtle.

The changing room of a village cricket team before the start of play is like nothing else on earth. This is where the skipper plans his strategy, delivers his team-talk and gives his openers their instructions: "They've a strong batting side. So we need six an over. Oh, and, whatever you do, don't get out. We can't afford to lose any early wickets." Simple, sensible stuff. Before the team goes out to field, he can remind them: "Remember, catches win matches." It is a sentiment we can all share – until the first catch goes down, and we have to face the fact that if we do manage to win it will be despite, not because of, our catching.

THE DISTINCTION BETWEEN TACTICAL DISCUSSION
AND BOOZE-UP IS VERY SUBTLE ...

The changing room is where team camaraderie is forged; where the players bond together, instilling mutual self-belief as they mull over the previous week's game. If a batsman was run out, he can be given helpful advice ("Linford Christie wouldn't have gone for that run"). If he failed to get off the mark, he can have his confidence boosted by an innocent inquiry: "How many was it you made last week?"

"I want players to prepare in the way they like best," Nasser Hussain said when he took over the England captaincy. We know exactly where he is coming from. Each member of our team prepares for the game in his own way, with a routine – tried and tested over the years – that works for him. We attach as much importance to psychological preparation as we do to physical fitness. The players use a range of sophisticated techniques tailored to the needs of the individual: a quick cat-nap in the corner to catch up on lost sleep; a few furious puffs on a

cigarette; draining the last dregs of the pre-match beer; telling a joke that no one else finds funny; checking on the results of the two o'clock at Kempton Park; spraying some obnoxious compound, allegedly good for toning up the muscles, onto himself (and the rest of the team). Little things, but they can make all the difference.

After the game, the average changing room has a good deal in common with Brighton beach at the end of a Bank Holiday weekend. Discarded socks with unspeakable smells; plastic bags containing who knows what; half-eaten apples; congealed pieces of chewing gum stuck to the window-sill; squashed beer cans; cigarette ends; jock-straps; sweaters that must once, very long ago, have been white; towels too soggy to investigate; odd boots clogged with mud.

*   *   *

For many years our club's social highlight was a dance held, half-way through the season, in a large tent, always referred to as 'the marquee'. Sod's law dictated that the mid-summer Saturday earmarked for this grand event was often the wettest night of the year. The formula was always the same: live music (loud and of variable quality), food (mediocre), and booze (excellent). Our committee is not perfect, but it does have a good understanding of the players' priorities.

When the pubs had closed and the gatekeeper had gone home, the marquee proved an irresistible attraction to local youngsters looking for half an hour of mayhem to round off the evening. On one occasion things got out of hand. The final straw came, almost literally, when one of the gatecrashers decided that things needed hotting-up. He set about lighting a fire in front of the makeshift stage where the band were performing. As the stage was supported on bales of straw, we decided that this was not a very good idea. Prevented in the nick of time from sending the marquee and everyone in it up in flames, he shinnied to the top of the central pole and beamed down at the dancers below. A small figure high above the crowd, he put me in mind of a skylark perched on a telegraph pole – until he began to sing. It was a strange, strangulated voice, more farmyard than opera house. Most of the words were slurred and unintelligible. Unfortunately, when it came to the final, most obscene verse, he got a second wind and the words rang out clear as a bell. He made a great impression, but it was the last of our marquee dances. The committee, in its infinite wisdom, decided that enough was enough.

*   *   *

Village cricketers may not take much interest in politics, but they have to admit that Governments have done at least two useful things in the last forty years. The introduction of the early May Bank Holiday added another precious day to the cricket calendar of many village clubs; and relaxation of the licensing laws, allowing refreshment to be taken not only before and after, but also during, a match, helped to sustain one of the game's very oldest traditions.

The Royal Family has shown its support for the game by

ensuring that public holidays to celebrate its weddings and jubilees fall during the cricket season. The Golden Jubilee of 2002 presented us with a problem. Our star opening batsman had to be in two places at the same time, combining his duties on the cricket field with his role as master of ceremonies at a children's carnival. A consummate professional, he solved this problem with effortless ease, getting himself out, clean bowled, for a duck in both innings of a two innings game. A fine example to us all. We celebrated the Silver Jubilee of 1977 in similar style. It is remembered in our village not for the Royal Procession down the Mall, but for the procession of batsmen who went out to the middle and returned to the pavilion without having made any contribution to the score. To this day, the start of our innings – no runs for six wickets – remains a club record.

Another memorable match was a sponsored game, in aid of a local charity, against a Showbiz Eleven. Usually our spectators can be counted on the fingers of one hand; but on this occasion, the good cause and the promise of well-known personalities attracted a presentable crowd. Our opponents were "celebrities" from the world of music and broadcasting – disc jockeys, producers, sound engineers and so on. They all had just one thing in common: every one of them, without exception, was totally unknown.

We had organised special catering facilities and, like the sponsors' tents at Lord's, these were of more interest to some spectators than the cricket. But it was the same in cricket's early days. In the 18th century, important matches, like that between Hambledon and England at Guildford in 1772, always had their refreshment booths (some rented by the nobility), and the publicans who ran them did excellent business.

Our visitors made an immediate impression when their tannoy system erupted without warning, startling the more elderly spectators out of their skins. Luckily there were no heart attacks. A blast of pop music was followed by the gratingly cheerful voice of a disc jockey. He obviously knew that the crowd had come not to enjoy the quiet pleasures of a country cricket match, but to be entertained with wall-to-wall pop music and a barrage of inane prattle. He announced the names of the Showbiz Eleven, giving a potted biography of each player, complete with references to obscure pop records and radio programmes no one had heard of. Eventually this subsided and the two umpires walked out to the middle, followed by the Showbiz fielders and, bringing up the rear, our two opening batsmen. It was an all-day game, and neither my partner nor I was used to such an early start. We were going out to bat at a time when we should have been making a leisurely start to the day over the Sunday newspapers.

On reaching the wicket, I took guard and looked around at the field placings. This was the 1970s, and the flared whites of the Showbiz Eleven cut quite a dash. I settled down to face the first delivery. The bowler went back to his mark, turned and started his run-up. As he arrived at the crease and released the ball, the tannoy erupted with another blast of music. This was followed almost immediately by a loud and unnecessarily jubilant announcement: "And already the Showbiz Eleven have taken their first wicket."

The day ended memorably, with both teams being invited back to our president's house for supper. As we tucked into our supper, one of our players, a young man whose talent at the crease was eclipsed by an even greater talent for shifting pint after pint of Guinness, took the opportunity to demonstrate a dexterity and synchrony of movement our players rarely achieve on the cricket field. With perfect coordination of eye, hand and body, he simultaneously knocked back a tumblerful of gin and knocked over a priceless piece of porcelain.

Eating and drinking have always been an essential part of cricket – often more important than the game itself. Even at the famous Hambledon Club, cricket was played only by a minority of the members. The club's central purpose was always the entertainment of its members by weekly "meetings", with ample food and drink. Many years ago Newport (Salop) set a fine example when, playing against "Will o' the Wisps" at Trentham Park in Staffordshire, they returned home without completing the match in protest at the inadequacy of the refreshments provided. All they had been offered was "a hamper containing four ducks, four fowls, eight bottles of wine and a large bottle of ale". Some first class cricketers have also done their best to uphold standards. The Notts player George Gunn was batting in a match at Leicester when the clock reached one-thirty and he turned towards the pavilion, only to have his movement interrupted by the umpire, who said "we have our lunch at two o'clock." When Gunn received the first ball of the next over he walked down the pitch and made no attempt to play it. He was stumped by yards. "*I* have my lunch at one-thirty," he said to the umpire as he went back to the pavilion.

* * *

Our village cricket club was established, so older members had always said, "around the turn of the century." With many local clubs celebrating their centenaries, we set about establishing the precise year of our birth. One of our members took it upon himself to do some serious research. He contacted the local newspapers, visited the county reference library, and wrote up the results of his research. This was time-consuming work, and by the time 1875 was identified as the all-important year, the centenary had passed us by and we had almost reached our 125th anniversary.

We celebrated this in style. The central event was a six-a-side competition involving both past and present players. Only when it was too late did we realise that six-a-side cricket has one big snag: there just six players on each side. This is fine when your team is batting, but not so good when you are fielding. With one bowler and one player behind the stumps, you are left with just two fielders on either side of the pitch. Patrolling an outfield in an eleven-a-side match is difficult enough; when you have just six, and when two of those are former players looking as if they have left their zimmer frames at home, you have your work cut out. Once the downside of six-a-side cricket had become apparent, we were quick to grasp the one great advantage of a knock-out competition: the ease with which, as soon as you are knocked out, you can put your feet up and watch the proceedings from the comfort of the pavilion. So the competition – not to reach the final, but to be knocked out ASAP – was cut-throat.

*   *   *

In village cricket, it is customary for any player who makes fifty runs or takes five wickets in an innings to buy a jug of beer. For many of us, this custom is of little more than academic interest, but there is an interesting paradox – an inverse relationship between a player's talent and his willingness to pay up. A cricketer whose performance on the cricket field is razor-sharp usually has slug-like reactions when it comes to putting his hand into his pocket.

For the treasurer and many of our players, the club's social calendar is far more important than the fixture list. Over the years we have organised all manner of events: line-dancing, disco-dancing, karaoke, horse-racing (not on the cricket field, but on a video screen) and – perhaps most popular of all – ferret-racing. But they are all based on the activities with which cricket has always been associated: dancing, betting, singing and, of course, drinking. Long ago, when our players were younger and had small children, we used to celebrate the Fifth of November with a bonfire and fireworks.

This gave Basil, one of the club's all-time heroes, a bright idea. He took it into his head to clear up the pavilion and ground and to make a bonfire of the surplus rubbish. Only when it was too late was it discovered that Basil's definition of rubbish included the club's early scorebooks. 'Rubbish' would have been a perfectly accurate description of many of the performances recorded there; but sending them up in smoke was a clumsy way of rewriting history. In fact, Basil was only following the example set by two of our most famous public schools. In 1825, some boys from Eton and Harrow (having had a little too much to drink), set fire to the pavilion at Lord's and destroyed most of the MCC's scorebooks.

Chapter 14

Going on Tour

A cricketer setting off on tour feels like a schoolboy on the first day of the summer holidays.

But five days of cricket can come as a shock when all the body is used to is a few hours on a Saturday afternoon. Self-discipline is the key, and the right kind of preparation is vital. The modern cricketer on tour starts the day with a mile-long jog. He then showers and has a light breakfast of orange juice, muesli and fresh fruit, washed down with a small cup of decaffeinated coffee. After that comes a rigorous work-out in the nets, perhaps followed by a team meeting to discuss tactics. The morning is rounded off with a light lunch – tuna salad, say, accompanied by a slice of wholemeal bread and a glass of mineral water.

Village teams on tour do not, thank God, include any modern cricketers. Their start to the day is in an older, more forgiving tradition. It begins with the players sleep-walking their way down to breakfast, looking as if they have been put through an old fashioned mangle. Then they manfully pull themselves together to tackle a full English breakfast of eggs, bacon, mushrooms, tomatoes and fried bread, rounded off with four or five slices of toast with lashings of strawberry jam. All this is washed down with a giant mug of tea, into which the average player shovels three teaspoonfuls of sugar, and consumed to the accompaniment of assorted burps and other, more noxious, emissions.

With the first half of the morning taken care of, the second half can be given over to some serious preparation: a round of golf, perhaps, followed by a round of drinks in the clubhouse. Between the full English breakfast and the extravagant tea that most clubs feel obliged to provide for a team on tour, the players can squeeze in a light lunch: a steak sandwich, perhaps, with a double portion of chips, washed down with three or four pints of beer.

Tea is a vital component of any cricket match, but on tour, it is often the be-all and end-all. Most clubs entertaining a touring side go out of their way to provide a good tea, perhaps believing that, with all the cricket they play and all the drinking they do, they need feeding. Some go overboard, like one club in the West Country. The table was heaving with cold meats, sausages, cheeses, French bread, lettuce, radishes, spring onions, tomatoes, celery, gherkins, pickled onions; home-made cakes, bulging with cream; and, to finish off, strawberries or fresh fruit salad. A cricketer needs to be on top form to get through this lot, but it is surprising what he can do when he has to. Allowances can be made for a touring side which, through over-indulgence the previous evening, fails to give the home team a decent game. What will never be forgiven is a touring side that fails to do justice to the tea.

The first challenge of any tour is for the players to get themselves to the right place, at the right time, for the first match. Hire of a coach or minibus would be the simplest solution, but this is far too simple for a team of free spirits who prefer to drift down, as and when it suits them, under their own steam. Our standard routine is a lunch-time rendezvous at whichever pub is closest to the ground.

One friend drives down sedately in his battered old saloon at a maximum of fifty miles an hour, ignoring the column of frustrated drivers behind him. Another does his best to set a land speed record for getting from A to B. Those who want to make the most of the journey meander down, stopping off randomly at any town or village that catches the eye, and taking the opportunity for a little light refreshment en route. Anyone prepared to take a little trouble can often unearth unexpected treasures: the smallest town can hide a surprising number of pubs.

*   *   *

Every year, on principle, we go to a different part of the country. It is an annual mystery tour, a leap into the unknown. As tour manager, I have occasionally found time for a brief reconnaissance visit. The first priority is to check out any pubs which might be suitable as the team's HQ. This involves extensive research, which always takes much longer than planned and usually leaves no time to take a look at the grounds where we will be playing.

So, finding the ground can be a problem. Directions provided by the home team are often susceptible to more than one interpretation. If our team is travelling in half a dozen different cars, the likelihood of all of them making it to the ground in time for the start of play is pretty remote. On tour one year in Wiltshire, we were going in convoy from our HQ to the first match. We drove through a deserted village and out again into the open country without seeing any sign of a cricket ground. We reversed our cars and went back through the village. Eventually we spotted the ground; it was hidden behind the hedgerow that ran alongside the road. We could see the cricket field, but not how to get into it. At length we discovered a small gap in the hedge, where a rough track left the road, crossed a narrow ditch, and entered the ground. Five of our six cars navigated this gap successfully. The sixth, for reasons that were never satisfactorily explained, missed the gap in the hedge – but found the ditch.

The car was a clapped out old banger, an Austin maxi; it had done pretty well to get all the way from Buckinghamshire to Wiltshire. After getting so close, it was a shame that it fell at the very last hurdle. The car's owner, who had recently embarked upon an economy drive involving non-renewal of his AA subscription, set off in search of the local garage. He was gone for some time.

Later that afternoon the car provided an absorbing spectacle as it was slowly winched out of the ditch. It was far more compelling than anything that was happening on the cricket field. The car slithered and struggled, as if being in the ditch suited it better than being on the road. At length it was freed from the brambles, lifted clear of the ditch and manoeuvred onto the rescue lorry. The car was in a bad enough state when it went into the ditch, but it emerged looking a good deal worse: a shattered windscreen, a flapping exhaust pipe and several new dents in the bodywork. And that was just what we could see from a distance of 100 yards or so. Heaven knows how much mechanical damage there was. As the car disappeared down the lane, its owner watched it go, a strange expression on his face. I'm not sure whether it was love or hatred. He changed into his cricket gear and came out onto the field, just in time to join us as we came off for tea.

* * *

Mishaps with cars are a routine hazard of our cricket tours. On tour in North Devon, I located our rendezvous and, the car park being full, found a space opposite the pub in the high street. Half an hour later I went back out to the car to retrieve my directions to the ground. I unlocked the door and reached across into the glove compartment.

This is where Sod's law came into play. I had parked the car adjacent to a telegraph pole. As I knelt on the driver's seat, searching for the piece of paper I needed, the door swung open and the telegraph pole neatly scythed through the key that I had left in the door lock. It took the head of the key clean off, leaving the severed barrel inside the lock. If I had set out to do this, it would have taken a great deal of skill. I would have had to park the car at precisely the right distance from the telegraph pole, and at just the right angle – too close, and the door, rather than the key, would have been caught by the pole; too far away and the key would have missed the pole. Yet, I had managed it quite effortlessly, with instinctive, inch-perfect judgement.

When something embarrassing happens to a cricketer, news spreads through the team like wildfire. In an instant, half a dozen figures were bent over my car door. At first, I thought they were inspecting the damage but when I looked more closely, I saw that they had just creased up laughing.

We embarked upon some intricate key-hole surgery. It was a delicate operation, involving all manner of sophisticated instruments: penknife, match-stick, screwdriver, tweezers, and a piece of metal for screwing studs into the sole of a cricket boot. Eventually this resourcefulness paid dividends, as the broken key was extracted from the car door. But our triumph was short-lived. Hard as we tried, coaxing the broken key into the ignition lock was just impossible. There was nothing for it but to abandon the car. It was retrieved at the end of the week, thanks to a player who, joining us for the last game of the tour, brought down the spare car key I had thoughtfully left at home. But it's an ill wind that blows nobody any good. Without a car, I was unable to drive. And being unable to drive, I **was** able to drink.

*   *   *

But the most spectacular start of all to any of our cricket tours was provided by my 2CV, a car that occupies a unique place in the annals of our club's history. We were en route to Lincolnshire, and I had bravely offered a lift to the friend who had had such spectacular success, two or three years earlier, opening and closing the car's flap window.

We had stopped off at my son's house in Leicester for a coffee, and had left the city behind us when I became aware of the vague whiff of burning. After a moment or two, the smell seemed to disappear. Perhaps I had imagined it. Perhaps there had been some minor problem that had corrected itself. No cause for concern. But a few minutes later the smell was back, and this time there was no mistaking it. The 2CV is an idiosyncratic little car, but when a curl of smoke seeps out from beneath the dashboard, it is a fair bet that something is not quite as it should be.

I pulled up, put the warnings lights on, and got out to investigate. As I opened the bonnet, a puff of smoke hit my spectacles. When I had given them a wipe I saw that the smoke was coming from somewhere beneath the engine. Within a second or two it had thickened into a continuous black stream. At this point, my travelling companion decided to help. He came round to the front of the car and stuck his head under the bonnet. A moment

later he removed it – as a small flame burst out from beneath the smoke – just in time to avoid combustion.

By this time, the 2CV had become a tourist attraction. We were on the A46 and the stretch of road where this drama was unfolding was not a dual carriageway. I had turned it into a single track road, and heavy streams of traffic were building up in both directions. A smouldering 2CV must have provided an entertaining spectacle to drivers compelled to slow down to a crawl.

At this point, reinforcements came riding over the horizon. Two cars carrying four other members of our team had been travelling a mile or two behind – perhaps suspecting that my accident-prone passenger and the 2CV were not the best of combinations. They pulled up a safe distance away and rushed to lend their assistance. One of them joined me in trying to extinguish what was now a rather large flame. We grabbed a carpet from the boot and used it to beat down the flame, trying to smother the fire. A second used his mobile phone to call the fire brigade. The other two went out into the road, posted themselves on either side of the 2CV, and turned themselves into traffic policemen, allowing vehicles to pass alternately from each direction. We may not be much of a cricket team, but when it comes to a car going up in flames, we can turn ourselves into quite a professional outfit.

But our fire-fighting efforts were not a great success. The harder we beat the flame, the more fiercely it blazed, and within a couple of minutes the fire was out of control. We scrambled round to the back and managed to get our cricket gear out of the boot in the nick of time. A moment later the flame reached the soft, plastic roof of the car. In an instant it was gone, shrivelled and melted into air. Seconds later there was an explosion as the fire reached the petrol tank.

By the time the fire engine arrived, the 2CV was just an empty shell. The cremation was almost complete: it could not have had a more spectacular send-off.

The whole incident, from the first sniff of smoke to an enforced and rather protracted discussion with the local constabulary, took less than an hour, and we arrived at the venue for our first game in time for the scheduled start of play. There was even time for a recuperative pint of beer. The tour had got off to an excellent start.

* * *

Our first ever tour was a weekend foray into Dorset. There were just two games, and they provided an interesting contrast. The first was against a club one of our players had played for before he moved up to Buckinghamshire, and we played the club's second eleven. But on that particular Saturday the club's first eleven had been decimated by a wedding. Why any cricketer should ever choose to get married on a Saturday, when he could be playing cricket, is one of life's unfathomable mysteries. As a result, most of the club's second eleven had been dragooned into playing for the firsts. The knock-on effect of this was that any resemblance between the collection of individuals who took the field against us and a cricket team was purely accidental. Some teams make up in enthusiasm what they lack in skill: not this one.

We began in the field, and within ten minutes, we had dismissed the first four batsmen. We huddled together to discuss tactics (or perhaps it was to keep warm: it was a dull, miserable day, not cricket weather at all). "Making a game of it" was considered for all of five seconds before we reached unanimous agreement on a cunning tactical plan: "Let's get it over with, and into the pub".

Our game on the Sunday was a different affair altogether. It was against a club described by its fixture secretary as a "village" team. But there are village teams and village teams. This village team had two beefy opening batsmen, both of whom scored hundreds, and a Hampshire colt who, some 20 years later, remains the fastest bowler I have ever faced. He went through our team like a knife through butter. After the game the opposition skipper, magnanimous in victory, charmed us with his tact and diplomacy: "Of course, he wasn't bowling flat out today. Only a friendly. He's quite a handful when he bends his back."

So on that first tour we had two one-sided, pretty awful games. Yet, the tour was unanimously declared a great success. This may have had something to do with a pub landlord whose flexible interpretation of the licensing laws and diligence in administering to the needs of a thirsty team were quite outstanding. After all, the least important part of any cricket tour is the cricket.

*   *   *

Every touring team has one. During the day, he may be the most congenial of companions; but at night he is deadly. When it comes to sorting out the rooming arrangements, he is treated like the fat schoolboy who is a liability to any team, always the last one to be chosen. Nobody wants him.

Who is he, this pariah? The loudmouth, who has little to say that is worth hearing, but never allows this to prevent him from saying it? The hay fever sufferer, who erupts with an explosion of sneezing just as everyone else is dropping off to sleep? The night owl, who turns in only when his room-mates are fast asleep, and whose ablutions sound like a jumbo jet landing at Heathrow? The over-imbiber, whose night is spent dashing from bed to bathroom, to the accompaniment of horrible sounds and unspeakable smells?

Familiar characters, all of them. Every touring team has them. But there is someone worse than any of these. Someone who can single-handedly wreak more havoc than the fastest opposition bowler, the most potent alcoholic concoction or even the fiercest curry. Someone whose impact is unremitting and inescapable: the snorer.

Not all snores are the same. They can be loud or soft, tuneful or tuneless, rhythmic or fitful, booming or shrill, melodious or staccato, deep or shallow. Some can be tolerated more than others. The sound made by our team's number one snorer is unique: a loud, reverberative crackle, like the rat-a-tat-tat of automatic gun-fire. After a couple of nights' exposure, his room-mates are in a sorry state, totally useless on the cricket field.

And there is no easy remedy. You can wake the snorer up by giving him a gentle, or a not-so-gentle shake, or by throwing something at him. The trouble is, he only falls asleep again, and within a second or two he has resumed his sound attack with even more vigour than before. You can move into the next room, if you don't mind sleeping on the floor. But the walls of most hotel bedrooms are notoriously flimsy; and, faced with a thorough-going, professional snorer, even a solid Victorian wall is no guarantee of peace. One of our players who has suffered more than most has tried everything, from alcohol to sleeping tablets. At the end of our last tour he was at his wits' end, a broken man, and he decided to do some serious research. He believes he has found an answer: ear plugs. Next year we shall see whether or not he is right. Has he cracked it, or will our champion snorer rise to the challenge?

Chapter 15

Surviving the Tour

Most cricketers like a pint or two of beer after the match. On tour in Kent, however, we came upon a team who liked to round off a day in the field not with beer, but with port. No, that's not quite right ... they started with beer and went on to port. Or, perhaps they started with port and went on to beer? I can't quite remember.

Port and beer is an interesting combination, especially if you are not used to it. It was one of those rare days when I had managed to score a few runs, so I didn't need much persuading to enter into the spirit of things. Our opponents (a team of rugby players) were good cricketers, but they did not believe in exerting themselves unduly on the cricket field. They preferred to save themselves for the more important shenanigans after the game. That was when the real competition began and, as honoured guests, we were invited to participate. Something about the body language of the prop forward who issued the invitation suggested that, all things considered, it would not be a good idea to refuse.

The first challenge was a crisp-eating contest. Each team chose a champion, and they went head-to-head to see which of them could devour a packet of crisps in the shortest time. Our man was a thirsty farm-worker. When we played at home, he was noted for arriving late, leaving early, and disappearing at odd intervals to feed his pigs. He had recently given up farm work and gone to university as a mature student. There, he had discovered sex.

He had brought his girlfriend along with him, and he was evidently using the cricket tour as a test laboratory. The first to retire in the evening and the last to appear at breakfast, he was determined to give his new-found discovery a rigorous trial. He was knackered before he stepped onto the cricket field, and by the end of the week he was a physical wreck.

While we were batting, he spent his time sauntering around the boundary hand-in-hand with his girlfriend, disappearing from time to time into the long grass. He was a bowler who liked to bang the ball in short of a length. Now and again, if there was a bit of bounce, he could be a handful; more often, he went for a lot of runs in a short space of time. He did manage half a dozen overs, which doesn't sound too bad considering his extra-curricular activities. It would have been even better if it had been achieved during that one game, rather than over the five days of the tour.

A fierce competitor, he had honed his crisp-eating skills in the pubs of Buckinghamshire and Aberystwyth. But his off-the-field exertions had taken their toll, and his body reacted sluggishly to the challenge. Our opponents' man was home and dry, bag of crisps demolished, with several seconds to spare. One nil to the opposition. Our champion retired, humiliated, to the back of the pavilion. His girlfriend steered him towards a dark corner where she did her best to revive his spirits and massage his ego (and, perhaps, other bits of him).

The second challenge was for men of more sophisticated tastes. The objective was to keep a double brandy in the mouth, without swallowing it, for the longest period of time. Again, two champions were put head to head. Our man was a rotund farmer with a lot of experience under his belt. The timekeeper gave them a countdown, and they were off, heads thrown back and brandy glasses drained. Soon their faces were red and their cheeks blown out, as the brandy burned the inside of their mouths. But our champion was doing well; he was in better shape than his opponent, whose supporters were looking worried. Our man's cheeks were blown out like a balloon, but he looked comfortable. A moment later his opponent spluttered and swallowed his brandy, conceding defeat.

It was only after our man had been declared the winner that he was discovered to have broken the rules. Instead of keeping

the brandy in his mouth, he had allowed it to slip surreptitiously down his throat. His blown-out cheeks, convincing
everyone that the brandy was still in the mouth, had been
simple play-acting. All's fair in love and war – and in cricket.
His victory was allowed to stand.

With one victory apiece, a game of "stumps" was agreed
upon to decide the rubber. This is a simple game. The two
teams are lined up side by side, each player armed with half a
pint of beer. About ten yards in front of each team, a single
stump is stuck into the ground. As soon as the referee shouts
"go!" the first player sinks his beer, runs to the stump, places
both hands on top of the stump and his head on top of his
hands, and in this position completes three circles of the stump
before running back to touch the next player, who goes through
the same rigmarole – and so on until each member of the team
has done the same. The team to finish first is the winner.

When it came to my turn, knocking back half a pint of beer
and running out to the stump was easy. Completing three
circles, with my hands on the stump and my head touching my
hands, was slightly more difficult – but I managed it, albeit
more slowly than most. The real problem came on the return leg
as I set off, a little unsteadily perhaps, for home. Suddenly the
ground was no longer horizontal under my feet. It was slanting
upwards at an acute angle, and every time I put one foot in front
of the other, it moved violently and changed position.

Staying on my feet and running in a straight line was not
easy. I took a series of wild zigzags, tacking backwards and
forwards like a sailing boat trying to make headway against a
strong wind. It was touch and go, but I managed to stay on my
feet until I was within a couple of yards of our team. Then I
crashed to the ground, taking the next man in line down with
me as I collapsed over the starting line. He disentangled
himself, picked himself up, and set off at a frantic pace, determined to make up the ground I had lost. Some hope.

We put up a valiant fight, but we were no match for a bunch
of rugby players. For them, stumps was just a gentle prelude
before they got down to some serious horseplay. We had neither

the stamina nor, thanks to the port, the stomach for anything more. We said our goodbyes and tried to remember where the car park was. Then we broke into an impromptu, schoolboy race to see who could get there first. We had six cars and their drivers (a gallant mixture of supporters and players who had remained soberly aloof from the post-match shindig) looked on in bemusement. Adrenalin (or possibly port) flowing, I set off at a sprint, making only the slightest of detours to swoop down on my unfinished glass of beer, scoop it up and polish it off en route without any perceptible slackening of pace. This required consummate skill: perfect coordination of hand and eye, something every cricketer needs. Picking up a beer glass, well, it's instinctive. Applying the same skill to get bat on ball is a different matter altogether.

The drive from our hotel to the ground had taken some 45 minutes, but the return journey was much quicker. No sooner had I got into the back seat of the car, than I found myself clambering out and stumbling into the hotel lobby. I walked unsteadily up to the reception desk and asked for my key. The words seemed to have some difficulty getting out of my mouth in the correct order. The receptionist glared at me with the kind of look receptionists everywhere reserve for guests who are not quite up to the hotel's standards.

At length I succeeded in making myself understood and the receptionist disappeared into his cubby hole. When he emerged with the key, the space above the reception desk, where my face had been, was empty. My legs had given way and I had slumped to the floor. He peered over the desk and looked down at me. He had a strange expression on his face. It *could* have been a look of sympathy, but I wouldn't want to bet on it.

My sudden subsidence was a perfect climax to the day's entertainment...or so my team-mates thought. It was some time before they could stop laughing and pull themselves together sufficiently to help me onto my feet, up the stairs and into my room. I collapsed onto the bed and looked up at the ceiling: it began to rotate, going round and round, and getting faster and faster. Then it spun out of control.

* * *

Why the hell doesn't the batsman put bat to ball? Step out and hit the bloody thing, instead of prodding about like an old woman, dabbing it here and there, giving it respect it doesn't deserve.

When you are sitting in the pavilion, waiting to go in, slow bowling is such a doddle. When you reach the crease, things are a bit different. The slow bowler who looked a piece of cake from the pavilion has actually found a pretty good length. He even gets the odd ball to turn a bit. In fact, when he gets everything right, he is quite a handful.

The slow bowler we came up against on tour in the West Country was more than a handful. He was a slow bowler in the sense that he spun the ball. In point of fact, his "slow" bowling was about the same speed as that of our fast bowlers. He was a leg-spinner – a pretty rare breed. Rarer still, he was an accurate leg-spinner, pitching ball after ball on a good length. What made him unplayable, though, was what the ball did when it hit the turf; it jumped up off the pitch like a fire-cracker, seemingly travelling faster than before it pitched. He was an Australian and I can't remember his name. I don't *think* it was Shane Warne, but I can't be sure.

* * *

The eastern half of England is drier than the west. Average rainfall is significantly lower. But averages can be misleading. My batting average, which has never reflected the quality of my batting, is a good example. So when we decided on a tour to Norfolk, it was only to be expected that Sod's law should precipitate one of the heaviest downpours in living memory.

Two games were washed out before they began; two games were abandoned after little more than an hour's play; and in the one game we managed to finish our skipper made what he subsequently described, with masterly understatement, as a small tactical error. We had reduced the opposition to something like 60 for 7, when he decided to open the game up. What he did not know was that the next man in, number 9, was a

top-order batsman who had turned up late. He monopolised the bowling and thumped the ball all around the ground. With dogged support from a number 11 who had just one (forward defensive) shot, he put on 80-odd runs and pushed the total up to over 150. We were then skittled out for less than 100.

The success of a cricket tour has very little to do with the weather. Some would even argue that there is an inverse relationship: the worse the weather and the less cricket there is, the more time can be spent in the pub and, therefore, the more successful the tour. Our week-long visit to north-west Norfolk was one of our toughest tours ever. It is hard work, putting back pint after pint, day after day after day.

Pub games can also test a team's stamina. Our champion performer is the hero who won the brandy-in-the-mouth contest. A pub game – any pub, any game – brings out his competitive streak. Instant metamorphosis. One moment he is a placid, unobtrusive soul, quietly sipping his beer in the corner. The next he is a ruthless, stop-at-nothing, winner-takes-all competitor. Crib, darts, dominoes, it's all the same to him. The pinnacle of his career came during a tour to Somerset, when he was introduced to skittles. His technique was straightforward and effective. What he lacked in skill, he made up for in ferociousness. He hurled each missile at the pins as if he was launching cannon balls at an enemy.

Our pub in Norfolk had both a pool table and a snooker table. These games might seem as far away from cricket as you can get, but they have one crucial thing in common: what you lack in skill, you can make up in tactical ingenuity. All you need is a partner who is on the same wavelength; one who understands the importance of tactics. Once you have built up an instinctive understanding, the possibilities are infinite. It's rather like a batting partnership, but far more satisfying because it's likely to last much longer. As with batting, timing is all-important. With practice, it becomes second-nature, any quiet remark to your partner automatically slipping out of your mouth at the precise moment when your opponent brings his cue into contact with the ball.

If your opponents are on a roll, keen to get on with the game as quickly as they can, a short discussion with your partner is the ideal way to slow things down. A long discussion can be even better. Psychological ploys like these sort out the men from the boys. There is no need to say anything relevant or interesting. In fact, the more boring it is, the better. A conversation about, say, your collection of old bus tickets or the life-cycle of the snail is ideal. If you can bore your opponents to death, you are almost home and dry.

When it is your turn to play, you need to think carefully, and at length, about your shot before you crouch down, get in line and prepare to strike the ball. Then, instead of pushing your cue onto the ball, you can withdraw and enter into a prolonged discussion with your partner which ends in an apparent decision to play a totally different shot. You then have to make elaborate preparations for the new shot, lining yourself up and lowering your chin in the approved manner until it almost touches the cue. But instead of striking the ball, you can have another change of heart and go back to your original shot. This routine can be repeated *ad nauseam* until your opponents have completely lost the plot.

We had one long and beautifully boring game of snooker against a pair of players whose tactics were less subtle than ours. It was played in the early hours of the morning, at the end of a long day, and our reactions were not what they might have been; we were a little slow on the uptake. While our opponents were at the table, my partner and I took the opportunity to refill our glasses. As one does. When it was my turn to play, I returned to the table and contemplated the layout of the balls. I could have sworn that one of the reds, which had not been disturbed by the last break, had looked a fairly easy pot. Now that I examined it more closely, it looked rather more difficult. Ten minutes later, a pot I had been convinced was "on" now looked as if it was on only if your name was Stephen Hendry. Then the reverse happened. One of our opponents was at the table, and a pot that had looked impossibly difficult a few moments earlier suddenly seemed the easiest shot in the world.

Suddenly the penny dropped and we cottoned on to what was happening. Whenever our backs were turned, our opponents were surreptitiously adjusting the positions of the balls. Not all of them, just one or two that were lying in crucial positions. Lesser players might have been riled by these tactics, but *we* took it as a compliment. It showed that our opponents were rattled and that our own, more subtle, game was working its magic.

* * *

Many cricketers play golf. In our team we have a couple of decent golfers, a lot of indifferent golfers, and me. My first problem is deciding which club to use. It takes quite a time to rummage through the bag, sort out which club is which, and decide which one to use. As if it made the slightest difference. However, the time spent in this way is not wasted. Far from it: it serves the very useful purpose of postponing the dreadful moment when the club has to make contact with the ball. Or not. When you play golf once a year, the chances of hitting the ball the first time you take a swing at it are pretty slim. Still, all is not lost. When you miss the ball, it is surprisingly easy to make your air shot look like a practice swing.

If my club hits anything, it is usually grass. My special talent is to bring the club down a couple of inches in front of the ball, tearing a nice chunk of turf out of the ground. If I do manage to make contact with the ball, the chances of it going in anything like the right direction are infinitesimal. There are three realistic possibilities: slicing the ball into the long grass or onto the fairway of a neighbouring hole; topping the ball, so that it skims over the grass like a stone over water; or getting under the ball, and watching it balloon up into the air and land a couple of yards in front of the tee.

The climax of my golfing career came during a tour to Gloucestershire. The course was idyllically situated, on the edge of the Cotswold escarpment. There were fine views. Or there would have been if our round of golf had not coincided with the onset of a storm. The wind got up just as we left the clubhouse. There was not much rain – just a few spots – but a dank mist came down and as we made our way round the course, it grew thicker. We struggled over the first few holes, getting slower and slower as it became more and more difficult to make out the pins. About halfway round, we were relieved to come upon a very short hole, with the flag clearly visible from the tee. For the first time I made excellent contact with the ball, hitting it bang in the middle and directly in line with the pin. It soared high into the air, where it was caught in a squall of wind. It was buffeted about and blown back over my head. It landed a few yards behind me, on the green of the previous hole.

The next day, the storm had abated sufficiently for us to play cricket. It was not until we were going out to field that a thick mist came down and the wind got up. It wouldn't have been so bad if the gale hadn't been blowing directly down the pitch. With the wind behind him, our opening fast bowler should have had a field day. The ball should have been swinging and seaming all over the place. But his first over was hopeless – perhaps the strong tail wind affected his delivery. Perhaps the conditions went to his head and he tried to bowl too fast. Whatever. It was an expensive, unproductive over, albeit an entertaining one. It's always nice to see a bowler losing his rag due to his own inability to put the ball in the right place.

The second over, into the wind, was even more entertaining. It was a stiff challenge – not for the batsman, but for the medium-paced bowler who struggled to get the ball from one end of the pitch to the other. His first two deliveries were caught by the wind and it was touch-and-go whether or not they would reach the batsman. After that, he settled for a low trajectory, pitching short of a length and giving the ball as little exposure to the wind as the conditions would allow. In this mode, he was our most economical bowler – and, since he took a wicket, our most successful.

A year or two later, mist came down as we were about to start a game in an out-of-the-way spot on the edge of Dartmoor. Our prelude to the game was some mushroom picking in the outfield. As things turned out, this was the high point of the afternoon. When we took to the field, the heavens opened and there was no question of play. We went into a huddle to decide how we should spend the afternoon. It took us some time to come up with an answer that everyone was happy with; oh, at least five seconds.

The pub was one of the strangest I have ever been in. It was perfectly suited to the desolate country – old, but not "olde worlde," the kind of pub that looks as if would really prefer not to have any customers at all. The beer, though, was good and came straight from the barrel behind the bar. Plain tables and chairs were arranged unceremoniously around two adjoining rooms. A third room, its door propped open behind an empty beer crate, smelt like the kitchen of a greasy spoon. Through the opened door we could see the end of a bed, and from here the landlady presided over proceedings. She had a thin voice, but one that sounded as if it was used to being obeyed. When her son behind the bar had poured our beer, she ordered us into her room. Bedridden and well into her nineties, she was, she said, the oldest landlady in the country. She chatted away to us, in an old nightie that had seen far better days, as if she had known us all her life. She was a merry old soul with twinkling eyes. Straight out of Dickens.

Another strange establishment was a restaurant we came

upon during a tour to Suffolk. Our meal began somewhat bizarrely when the manager (who doubled as the waiter, who doubled as the cook) greeted us with the news that everything on the menu was half the advertised price. The menu was quite extensive, but as we went through it, every dish we ordered was "off". Gradually it became clear that the only thing available was chicken. For a starter, there was a choice between chicken soup and hot chicken salad. This could be followed by a main course of roast chicken or chicken kiev or chicken risotto or grilled chicken or chicken ragout; or (if you wanted something a bit different), there was chicken tandoori or chicken tikka.

It transpired that the place had gone into bankruptcy, and the stock had all gone – except for the chicken, which the manager was desperate to get rid of. A couple of hours after we had left the restaurant and returned to our pub headquarters across the road, he walked into the bar carrying a cardboard box. He was sure we would want to round off the evening with a spot of supper – and he had just the thing.

*   *   *

One of the strangest grounds I have played on was in Devon. It was not easy to find. Eventually we discovered it hidden amongst sand dunes, at the bottom of a deep hollow, no more than a hundred yards from the shoreline. It was invisible until you were on it. Our opponents were another touring team, who turned up wearing an assortment of funny hats. They had a light-hearted approach to the game that misled us into thinking that they were not too bothered about winning. In retrospect, it's obvious that the headgear and the larking about were part of a carefully conceived tactical plan.

It was not easy for the players to know where the cricket field ended and the sand dunes began – and it was not just the cricketers who had this difficulty. The field was crossed on one side by a footpath that provided a short-cut to the beach. So when we were in the field, our forces were boosted from time-to-time by passing children and senior citizens with dogs. Our best fielder was probably a wire-haired fox terrier, adept at catching the ball after its first bounce. The batsman was never certain

whether the dog was going to release the ball straight away to a fielder or keep it in its mouth while it ran round and round in excitement. If it hung on to the ball, two or three runs were there for the taking; if it didn't, there was the risk of a run-out. With most batsmen opting for caution, the fox terrier saved us a lot of runs.

This ground in a goldfish bowl was not as much of an advantage to the fielding side as one might suppose. Bowlers not used to running in down a steep hill tended to trip over their own feet; while the fielders, not making sufficient allowance for the slope, suddenly discovered that the ground under their feet had disappeared. But it was not easy for the batsmen either. Anyone who played with a straight bat and tried to keep the ball on the ground had no chance of scoring runs. However hard he hit the ball, the slopes on all sides of the pitch soon slowed it down. The most he could hope for was a single. The best hope of a boundary was a rustic, cross-batted hoick across the line. So it suited us rather well.

* * *

Some years ago a team from Lincolnshire came down to play us.

Perhaps they knew that the early Hambledon cricketers were almost as famous for their singing as for their cricket. After the game, they entertained us to a tuneless but lusty rendition of *The Lincolnshire Poacher*. This brought back some happy memories. In the 1950s I had lived for two years in Louth, Lincolnshire, in a pub called *The Lincolnshire Poacher*, and it was here, as an eleven-year-old grammar school boy, that I first played cricket. So when I came to plan our tour for the following year, there was only one possible destination: Lincolnshire.

It was a remarkable tour. It had got off to a good start when the burnt out shell of my 2CV was abandoned on the A46, before we got anywhere near Lincolnshire. But, most of our tours have been marked by spectacular disasters of one kind or another, either on or off the field of play. This tour was memorable for something altogether more rare: a spectacular victory. It was against Skegness, a club as different from ours as a Ferrari is from a 2CV. The pavilion was large and well-appointed, with an upstairs bar and a balcony from which you could get a bird's eye view of play and pretend you were in the pavilion at Lord's. There was a huge, even outfield, into which our own cricket field would have fitted twice-over. The pitch was flat as a pancake. And, as if all this weren't enough, there was another small detail in which Skegness differed markedly from our own team: their players *looked* like cricketers. They even had an overseas professional, an obstreperous Australian.

Skegness won the toss and chose to bat. After losing an early wicket, they pushed rapidly ahead. A big partnership between one of the openers and their number three took the game just about out of our reach. The opener played very correctly, but punished anything the least bit wayward in length or direction. The number three was a stocky player, with a fondness for savage cuts and ferocious hits to leg. Time and again, he played across the line to good length balls, middling the ball and infuriating the bowlers. Our skipper looked around in desperation for someone to turn to. Clutching at straws, he ended up tossing the ball to the oldest player on the field: barely able to get his arm above shoulder height, he is the kind of chap who gives part-time bowlers a bad name.

He inspected the ball carefully and then rubbed the tips of his fingers over its surface, like a wizard trying to impart some magical properties to the ball. A total cod, of course. He took one leisurely pace forward and tossed the ball up towards the batsman. The stocky number three could have put it anywhere. He had plenty of time. Too much time. He didn't know whether to thump it over square leg for six, or to content himself with a four to deep point. He ended up doing neither. He was bowled by a gentle delivery that might just, on a difficult pitch and in very bad light, have troubled a nine-year-old.

This proved to be the turning point of the match. After that, wickets fell with satisfying regularity. Some of the batsmen were over-confident and took unnecessary risks; some had a bit of bad luck, like the opener who got an inside edge onto his wicket from a ball well outside the off stump; and, most amazingly of all, one (the number eleven) was beaten by a decent delivery when our opening fast bowler – totally ineffectual against the front-line batsmen – returned and proved just how unplayable he really was.

It was one of those rare, subliminal matches where everything goes right. This is difficult to handle when you are not used to it. Skegness were skittled out for a modest total, and we steered ourselves to victory with a few wickets and a few overs to spare. We, not Skegness, were the Lincolnshire poachers.

Chapter 16

Home or Away

Is Saturday's match at home, or away? It's the fixture secretary's job to know – and to make sure that everyone else knows. This sounds simple enough, but things are not always as simple as they seem.

One Saturday afternoon we arrived at the opposition's ground before the opposition. This was an unusual achievement: like most village teams, we are not renowned for our punctuality. A feather in our cap, we thought. But after a few minutes we stopped congratulating ourselves and started worrying. Then we went out to the middle: the pitch had neither been cut nor marked out. Suddenly someone had a brainwave. Perhaps there had been a balls-up? Perhaps the opposition had gone to our ground? So we bundled ourselves back into our cars and headed home.

When we got back to the ground, there was a note pinned to the door of our pavilion. It was from the opposition, saying they had returned home and would wait for us there. We must have passed them on the road somewhere between the two grounds. So we set off again in the opposite direction. By the time the two teams eventually met up and the pitch had been prepared for play, most of the afternoon was gone. It was far too late for the timed game we should have had. So we swallowed our principles and agreed to a limited overs thrash, fifteen eight-ball overs a side. Not proper cricket, but as good a way as any to work up a decent thirst.

*   *   *

Cricket grounds have their idiosyncrasies, just like cricketers. They are one of the charms of village cricket; no two grounds are the same. Take, for example, the boundary. It can come in all shapes and sizes, be made from all kinds of materials: white line, rope, markers or flags stuck into the ground, wooden fence, brick wall, road running along the edge of the cricket field, stream, ditch, hedgerow, wire-mesh, even barbed wire. The pitch too can vary enormously.

Most village pitches are slow, especially at the beginning of the season, and playing the ball too soon is a common way of getting out. Instead of going along the ground, the ball balloons up into the air. The slower the pitch, the greater the danger. Now and again, I have played on a pitch so soft and slow that it was touch-and-go whether or not the ball would reach the batsman. But I have not yet come across a ball as slow as the one encountered on W.G. Grace's first tour to Australia in 1873-74. When this ball pitched, it showed no inclination at all to bounce. It just stopped dead.

Once or twice a season we may, if we are lucky, play on a perfectly flat pitch. More often, the pitch is barely distinguishable from the outfield. It may be covered with grass; but there is grass and grass. Usually the stuff on the pitch is a rough-and-ready sort of grass, a hotchpotch of grass and weeds and strange, unidentifiable substances. When a batsman is playing on a bumpy pitch, especially in wet weather when the ball tears through the top as it pitches, he can use the time between each delivery to tap down the surface. But on one of the local grounds we play on, his time is better employed scouring the surface for little pieces of grit and stone. My prize find, a few years ago now, was a tiny piece of flint, with a sharp and shiny edge, embedded in the pitch just short of a good length. No wonder the opposition's bowlers, who play there week in, week out and know every blade of grass (and, perhaps, every piece of flint), habitually dig the ball in just short of a length. No use playing at home if you don't make the most of it.

* * *

Home advantage is very important in village cricket. It gives you a psychological advantage. You know what to expect, and you feel at home – unlike the England team at Lord's, reportedly made to feel on the outside of a club to which they don't belong.

A TiNY PiECE OF FLiNT – JUST SHORT OF
A GOOD LENGTH

A village team playing at home can put its competitive advantage to good use. When you know that your team will come off second best in a fair contest, you need to pull out all the stops to find ways of evening things up. So if you have a weak batting line-up, bringing the boundary line in a few yards further than usual, so that it is within easier reach of your batsmen, can make all the difference.

If, on the other hand, you have a decent batting line-up but bowlers who need all the help they can get, a simple remedy is at hand. All you need to do is to give your square some tender loving care. With the right kind of treatment a perfectly respectable pitch can be transformed overnight into 22 yards of spongy, bog-like turf, more suited to water polo than cricket. The first imperative is to forget to cut the pitch, so that you have a nice, thick covering of grass, at least half an inch longer than it should be. The second is to get the sprinkler out and turn the water on. And the third is to leave the sprinkler on (accidentally, of course) for at least 24 hours before the match. If conditions are exceptionally dry, you can leave it on even longer. If the sprinkler is turned off a couple of hours before the start of play, most of the water will be beneath (rather than on) the pitch, and the opposition will be none the wiser. Green on top, soft and moist beneath the surface, it will make a cricket ball do silly things. Your most innocuous bowler can be made to look half-decent and your medium-paced trundlers will be unplayable, transformed as if by magic into match-winners – if they can find a decent line and length. Admittedly – that's a pretty big if.

Local knowledge is all-important. If a village batsman plays on the same ground year after year, he knows how to make the most of it. He knows, for example, that if the ball is driven along the ground, the heavy outfield will slow it down long before it gets anywhere near the boundary. So he can use his experience to outsmart the fielders. If there is an upward slope towards the cover boundary, with tufts of impenetrable, overgrown grass, he knows that to have any chance of scoring more than a single he has to hit the ball in the air. For most village batsmen, hitting the ball in the air is something that comes quite naturally.

*   *   *

Most cricket grounds look fairly flat – from a distance. When you get close, however, things can look very different. The majority of village grounds are undulating to a greater or lesser extent, and some are about as flat as a camel's back. A player who has spent season after season playing on the same ground has a big advantage. He knows where the ground rises and falls, and he knows instinctively where to put his feet and how to keep his balance.

For the visiting team, things are not so simple. It is only when the fielder has to chase the ball to the boundary that he discovers all the charms of the outfield – the little hillocks, the patches of moss, and the hidden rabbit holes. The ground of one club we play against is on a heath. The outfield is a mass of thick, springy turf interspersed with tangled weeds and hidden potholes. A steepling catch can provide high entertainment. If the fielder keeps his eyes glued on the ball, it is a fair bet that his legs will give way under the uneven surface. If, on the other hand, he keeps looking down at the ground and so manages to avoid falling over, his chances of getting anywhere near the ball before it plummets to the ground are less than zero.

One ground we play on is perched on the Chiltern escarpment, high above the Vale of Aylesbury. The outfield falls away sharply towards one corner, and a shortish player fielding on the boundary at fine-leg or long-off has no chance of seeing what is happening at the far end of the pitch. The slope presents even more of a challenge to the bowler. At one end he has to struggle uphill until he is a couple of yards from the stumps, where the pitch flattens out abruptly onto a plateau. A bowler running in for the first time is often caught out by the need to re-adjust his stride. But this is child's play compared to the other end of the pitch. Here the bowler has to approach the pitch down a steep incline. Unless he slows down and checks his run-up as he reaches the wicket, he has a good chance of stumbling over and hurling himself, rather than the ball, onto the pitch.

*   *   *

Remember the school bike shed, and the shady characters who used to hang around it? With most children now being driven to school, it is past its heyday. But there is one place where it lives on, at least in spirit. Every village cricket ground needs its shed. It is a dark hole of a place, full of mysterious objects, strange substances and peculiar smells. To the groundsman, though, it is home, his inner sanctum. He may not (strictly speaking) own the shed, but possession is nine-tenths of the law and he is the proprietor of the premises as surely as if his name were displayed above the door like a pub landlord's. He may not have any formal power to prohibit players from going into the shed, but he can discourage them easily enough. It is one of the lesser known, but most widely applied, laws of cricket that the groundsman's shed must be kept in a state of perpetual chaos. In this way, he can make sure that no one else has the faintest idea where things are kept or how to find anything; and that any intruder has to navigate his way past a few strategically placed pieces of heavy machinery guaranteed to give him a bruised shin-bone.

Chapter 17

The Weaker Sex?

From W.G. Grace's mother to Geoff Boycott's girlfriend, women have been indispensable to cricket. Any village cricketer who has spent an evening on the telephone trying to get a team together knows just how important they are.

"Saturday, did you say? Yes, I'd love to play. [Loud eruption in background]. Hang on a minute, will you. [Silence, followed by raised voices, becoming increasingly agitated, followed by door slamming, followed by more silence]. Sorry, I'd better not. My back's been playing up, you know. I'd better not risk it."

Most of the office bearers listed on the club's fixture card may have men's names attached to them. But who is it who decides whether or not X is allowed to put himself forward for the committee? Who decides, early each spring, whether he has time to help the groundsman get the pitch prepared for the season – and, each autumn, whether he can help with the raking and loaming and re-seeding? Who decides whether he can spare the time to help redecorate the pavilion? Who decides, each week, whether or not he is allowed to play? Who decides how long he can stay on after the game has finished, enjoying a chat and a pint or two of beer? Who decides whether or not he can go on the club's annual tour?

Who is it who decides? When it comes to a rigorous manage-ment regime, the significant other of any village cricketer could teach the toughest company chairman a thing or two.

Our opening bowler fancies himself as a speed merchant. He psyches himself up and tears into the batsman with more belligerence than skill. After each delivery he glares down the pitch, giving a passable imitation of Glenn McGrath. Our number four batsman likes to make the close fielders quake in their shoes. He is not happy until he has bruised an ankle or two, and shown them who is in charge. Our all-rounder has an ego the size of his stomach, and in the pavilion after the game, his is the voice you can always hear.

At home things are very different. The fast bowler spends his Saturday morning scurrying around the garden, as his partner shouts her instructions from her chair in the kitchen. He finishes clipping the hedge and invites her to admire his handi-work. The line is not quite straight enough to satisfy her quality standards, and so he mutters something under his breath and goes over it again. And again. Meanwhile, the club's attacking batsman is dragging himself around the supermarket, working his way through a long list compiled by the management. He goes from one end of the store to the other and back again, back-wards and forwards like a yo-yo, grumbling and cursing as he searches for every last item. If he doesn't go home with the right kind of spaghetti, his life will be hell. The third member of our trio, the domineering all-rounder, has not been allowed out of the house. His wife has given him his orders. With family due to visit the next day, he finds himself skivvying up and down the stairs with the vacuum cleaner – a job that takes far more out of him than anything he is likely to do on the cricket field.

For all three players, domestic chores are part of the Satur-day morning routine. Each of them knows he has to earn plenty of brownie points so that they can be offset, later in the day, against the time he spends playing cricket. If he fails to get through what he has been told he must get through, he might just be able to skive off and get himself to the match in the nick of time. But his chances of being allowed to play the following week are less than his chances of winning the lottery.

* * *

When our team is desperate for players, anything goes. When things are bad, numbers eight to eleven in our batting order do not bear close scrutiny. On such occasions our number eight is a club member, called upon once or twice a season, who makes my five-year old grandson look like a cultured cricketer. Number nine is a natural number eleven, promoted above his station. It is ten years since he last picked up a cricket bat, and it shows. Our number ten is a schoolboy, with the makings of a decent cricketer – but not just yet. And number eleven is a woman.

A solitary woman in an otherwise all-male team can pose problems. Village clubs are not noted for the sophistication of their changing and toilet facilities. Some of our players can remember the days when the club, having no pavilion, used the village Guild Rooms. Former players can recall even earlier times when the hedge that runs along one side of the ground served as both changing room and latrine.

Nowadays almost all the clubs we play against have a pavilion with modern toilets and showers. But not all. I recently played against a team whose facilities had a feeling of the 1950s. After a fruitless search through the pavilion, I was advised to go "round the back". There, behind the pavilion, was a small lean-to shed with a corrugated iron roof. The door creaked as I opened it and looked inside; it was a dark, uninviting space with a distinctive odour. The basin was cracked and stained, and a piece of string hung down limply from the antiquated WC. The door bolt was rusted and would not be moved. It was not easy to attend to the business in hand while simultaneously keeping one foot jammed against the door.

Most village clubs have abandoned such primitive arrangements, but the provision of separate facilities for women is a different matter. Improvisation is the name of the game. If the pavilion has a bar, the dark recess behind the counter can provide a modicum of privacy. If she wants to be really popular, she can bolt the bar door and make thirsty players wait while she takes her time to make sure she is properly attired.

*   *   *

At Lord's, it took the MCC 212 years to admit women members. Things are different on the village green. Village cricketers know their limitations. They know that hard work and efficient organisation are phrases not automatically associated with the average club member. Those positions on our committee that require little more than the ability to bullshit are easy enough to fill. A job involving anything remotely like hard work is a different matter altogether. This is where our little club has the edge over our local rivals. Not only do we have a woman president, in recent years we have acquired both a woman secretary and a woman treasurer. So, the minutes of our committee meetings are circulated by Email the following day; the match fees and the bar takings are meticulously recorded; and the money is banked the very next day. We have been introduced to a whole new world.

We have gone even further, with the recruitment of two women scorers. When you consider the requirements of the job – a reasonable knowledge of the laws, a grasp of elementary arithmetic, an eye for detail – there really was no alternative. There was no chance of finding anyone among our playing members even remotely qualified. With their coloured pencils, their state of the art calculators and their handwriting that can actually be read, they have taken us into the 21st century.

* * *

Our club's annual tours have usually been men-only affairs. But one of the early ones, to Sussex, is still remembered for the prominent part played by a particular woman. Or was it women?

As the tour progressed it became clear that one of our players had organised his own individual social programme. Our first match was played on a common, with a road running along one side of the ground. We batted first, and half-way through our innings a car pulled up off the road and its occupant got out to watch the cricket. Or so we thought. It soon became clear that what she was really interested in was not the cricket, but the cricketers. She headed towards the group of players sprawled out in front of the pavilion. Before she had taken more than a few paces our wicket-keeper, always more successful at catching women than catching a cricket ball, sprung up and ran over to join her. Together they sauntered around the boundary. They found a seat on the far side of the ground and settled down to some serious canoodling.

The next day there was a repeat performance. Again the

young lady appeared in the middle of the game, and again our Don Juan escorted her to the furthest corner of the ground. There they stretched out on the grass and embarked upon an intimate one-to-one discussion. Probably our keeper was dissecting the technique of his opposite number out in the middle, sharing the finer points of his analysis with his girl-friend. But I could be mistaken.

Truth can sometimes be stranger than fiction. It may sound apocryphal, but the fact of the matter is that one of our players likes to combine his cricket with intermittent bird-watching. He really does. It so happened that on the afternoon in question he was admiring a herring gull that had landed on the outfield near the long leg boundary, when his binoculars strayed onto the pair of love-birds beyond the boundary. He let out a sharp exclamation of incredulity. After a moment or two he passed his binoculars around so that we could confirm what he had seen: the girl murmuring sweet nothings into the ear of our wicket-keeper was not the girl who had been with him the previous day.

Two days, two different girls. Before the next game there was a good deal of speculation. We could have run a book on the result. Who would it be today? A new one? Three girls in three days? Perhaps he had drawn up a matrix, with our fixtures along one axis and his girlfriends along the other, and matched them up alliteratively: Brenda in Brighton; Heather in Haywards Heath; Pauline in Pulborough; Christine in Crowborough; Rita in Rye.

As things turned out, there was no girl on the third day. It was a big let-down. But the next day, things looked up. There she was again. Our twitcher confirmed that it was girl number two, Tuesday's girl. Perhaps it was all over with girl number one? Perhaps we had been too hasty to draw conclusions. But on the next day, the last of our tour, we saw that we had not been too hasty at all. There she was. Only one thing was certain. It was not girl number two. Girl number two had shortish hair, very dark. This girl's hair was longer and not so dark. More like girl number one. And yet, there was something about her that was not quite the same. She kept her distance on the far side of a huge cricket field, and even the twitcher was unable to say for sure whether it was girl number one, back in favour after a short interlude, or a new girl. It was too close to call. A straw poll came down in favour of a new girl. That way, we had a much better story to tell when we got back home.

*   *   *

A few years ago, we had a woman player. Captain of a women's team that played on Sundays, she turned out for us on Saturdays. At the crease, she stood out like a sore thumb from the rest of the team – not because she was a woman, but because her shots were played very straight, with the full face of the bat. Not at all your average village cricketer, she had more style, if less brute force, than the rest of the team put together. But it was in the field that she really came into her own. She used to field at mid-off; easy on the eye and with the shortest of cricket skirts, she was worth at least a couple of wickets. After just one season with us, her work prevented her from playing more than one day a week and she had to choose between playing for us and playing for her women's team. Unaccountably, the women's team won.

Her departure left a void, but it was not long before one of our more enterprising members decided to fill the gap by organising some mixed cricket. This proved such a success that it has become an annual event. One evening, every July, our cricket field takes on a different character, as it is filled with players' wives, partners, girlfriends, sisters, daughters – and even one or two mothers.

A mixed cricket match is a fine spectacle. The men have to bat and bowl with their left hand – unless, of course, they are naturally left-handed, in which case they have to use the right. For many of us, it makes little or no difference which hand is used: when you don't succeed in getting bat on ball, it doesn't really matter whether the bat is in the left hand or the right hand.

Chapter 18

The Village Green

Does anything epitomise the peace and tranquillity of the English countryside better than cricket on the village green? A few acres of grass; cricketers in white; a pub; a church; a few spectators; and the best sound of an English summer – the crack of bat on ball. Perfect peace – broken only by a few traditional sounds. A hedge-trimmer zooming away in some nearby garden; rock music blaring out from a car radio; and the occasional Anglo-Saxon expletive from a player who is not having a good game.

The village green where one of our local rivals play their cricket is a chocolate box picture. Right in the middle of the village, it is surrounded on all four sides by cottages. From time to time, the cricket ball is hit into one of the cottage gardens. It is easy enough for a fielder to retrieve the ball – at least, it used to be. But this English idyll is not quite all it seems, for this village green has been fought over as fiercely as any patch of land since the English were at Agincourt.

The battle began when one of the residents took exception to cricketers coming into his front garden to retrieve the ball, and things rapidly got out of hand. What began as a little local difficulty escalated into a major dispute that hit the headlines of the local newspaper and even made the national press. Legal action was taken and eventually the case came to court.

The result was a nice English compromise. The cricket club was allowed to continue playing on the village green, on condition that netting was erected on match days to prevent the ball going into the residents' gardens. The logic behind this ruling was impeccable. What it failed to take account of, however, was the character of the average village batsman. Prohibited from

hitting the ball over the netting, how would you expect him to react?

It's the same in the nets. Their purpose is to prevent the ball going too far; but for many village batsmen the challenge is to hit the ball as far as they can out of the net – over the top, underneath the bottom, or back past the bowler. Some nets are well-maintained, with straight metal frames, strong netting and thick matting laid over a true, flat surface, giving a nice, consistent bounce. Others are like ours: a rusted metal frame supports a stringy, hole-infested net, held together by scores of home-made repairs. Hidden beneath a flimsy rubber mat that is past its sell-by date there is an uneven strip of concrete, from which ball after ball leaps up from a good length.

Net practice is a serious business. For any village club that takes its cricket seriously, the nets are a hive of activity. This is where, several evenings a week, the players practise for hour after hour, honing their skills; the batsmen trying out new shots and perfecting old ones, the bowlers striving for a good length and that nagging line around the off stump.

Perhaps some clubs have net practice like that. There is an alternative. It recognises that the important thing about net practice is to play in exactly the same way as you do out in the middle; and that the real purpose of the exercise is to work up a thirst in the shortest possible time before you retreat to the bar. So while the batsmen try to smash ball after ball back over the bowler's head, the bowlers bowl flat out, not minding too much whether the ball hits the stumps or the batsman.

*   *   *

In some villages, the cricket field also serves as a football pitch. The holes left by the goal-posts make a nice booby-trap for an unwary fielder, but it is the overlap between the cricket and football seasons that produces the most interesting results. It's not easy to play the first match of the season with one goalpost at square leg and another at long on.

What self-respecting footballer can be content with a mere nine months of football? Wall-to-wall football all the year round is what he wants – after all, a season almost twice as long as the cricket season is just not long enough. Some of our players are not too bothered about the increasing encroachment of football into the cricket season. It's not that they particularly like football: just that they are very happy to play as little cricket as decency will allow. But not everyone takes the same view. One of our members would like to see football banned, by law, from the beginning of May until the end of August, with stiff penalties for persistent offenders. If he had his way, capital punishment would not, I suspect, be ruled out.

It goes against the grain to admit it, but a few of our players play football as well as cricket. Two-timing in a big way. And not only that – when they are forced to make a choice between the two, cricket comes off second best. Always. The best we can hope for, if there is a clash of loyalties, is that the defector will come along to the cricket once his football is over. A player who has just spent 90 minutes running up and down a football pitch may be fagged out, but if he was fit enough to play football in the first place, compared to the rest of our team he will be in tip-top condition.

One ground we play on is large enough to accommodate both football and cricket. From the middle of August onwards, football is played alongside the cricket. On one side of the ground there is a keenly contested, end-to-end game. The players shout excitedly as they run up and down the field, jostling for the ball. On the other side of the ground, there is a cricket match. It's the difference between a wedding and a funeral. The spectators stand in a row along the touchline, watching the football. They have their backs to the cricket. Most of the cricketers, too, are more interested in the football than the cricket and, at the end of each over, they turn as one towards the football. It's as if the whole team, every man jack of them, are computer-controlled robots. When the bowler runs in to start the next over their eyes return, reluctantly, to the cricket.

An experienced fielder can even put the interval between each delivery to good use; he can spend far more time watching the football than playing cricket. He can judge to a tee the number of seconds he has free before he need pay attention to the cricket.

All village cricketers are pretty adept at this. Even when there is no football to watch. While the bowler plods back to the start of his run-up, the fielder has a few precious seconds when he can let his mind wander. He can lose himself in thought; work out what life is all about. He can forget all about the cricket – until the skipper's cry of "catch it!" brings him down to earth with a jolt. The ball may plummet to the ground before he can get anywhere near it – but what is a missed catch compared to the meaning of life?

Some cricket grounds are situated next to tennis courts or bowling greens. It is a safe bet that the rival sport (whatever it is) will attract more spectators than the cricket. Even a game of bowls. A cricket ball hit onto a bowling green can cause quite a stir. If it lands on the green and comes to a halt without touching any of the bowls, it is likely to be tossed back onto the cricket field. If, on the other hand, it happens to land on the bowls, so that it readjusts their positions, it may be a little more difficult for the cricketers to get their ball back. When cricket and bowls are played side by side, the cricketers and the bowls players, both in white, can be difficult to tell apart. But, there is a rough rule of thumb: the oldest ones are probably the cricketers.

One ground we play on is adjacent to the local golf course. Hitting the ball over the boundary and onto the golf course is a challenge some batsmen just cannot resist. It's not easy, but now and again someone manages to hit the ball onto the fairway – something that's often beyond the capabilities of the golfers, who seem to find it much easier to drive the ball onto the cricket field. A cricket ball on the fairway is picked up, sooner or later, by a golfer and thrown back onto the cricket field. A golf ball on the cricket field is a different matter altogether. However sluggish a fielder is when he is chasing a cricket ball, he can react with the speed of lightening when it comes to snitching a stray golf ball.

* * *

The village green is where it all began. In its early days cricket was a rough and tumble recreation enjoyed by farm workers when they had finished the day's labour. They gathered on the common land to relax and enjoy themselves. Many of their employers disapproved, believing that cricket was a pernicious influence, keeping men away from their work. In 1741, when a match in Buckinghamshire attracted a large crowd, one of the local landowners, Ralph Verney, described cricket as a "contagion".

How much have things really changed? Today, people who have spent the week in offices or factories, on tractors or on building sites, escape from the daily grind to spend a few hours in the open air – and a few more over a pint or two in the pavilion. And if only a minority of the players actually live in the village, that too is just as it was in the past. Many of the cricketers who played for Hambledon lived not in Hambledon itself, but in the surrounding towns and villages. Today's players may be salesmen and civil servants, barristers and builders – but at the weekend they, like their forebears of three hundred years ago, are just cricketers.

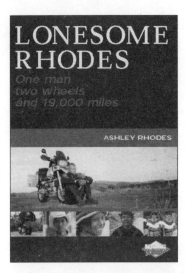
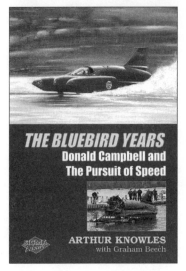